Building Private
Pension Systems

Number 6 in the ICEG Sector Studies Series

Since 1985 the International Center for Economic Growth, a nonprofit organization, has contributed to economic growth and human development in developing and post-socialist countries by strengthening the capacity of indigenous research institutes to provide leadership in policy debates. To accomplish this the Center sponsors a wide range of programs—including research, publications, conferences, seminars, and special projects advising governments—through a network of more than 230 correspondent institutes worldwide. The Center's research and publications program is organized around five series: Sector Studies; Country Studies; Studies in Human Development and Social Welfare; Occasional Papers; and Working Papers.

The Center is affiliated with the Institute for Contemporary Studies, and is headquartered in Panama with the administrative office in San Francisco, California.

For further information, please contact the International Center for Economic Growth, 243 Kearny Street, San Francisco, California, 94108, USA. Phone (415) 981-5353; Fax (415) 986-4878.

ICEG Board of Overseers

Building Private Pension Systems
A Handbook

Yves Guérard and Glenn Jenkins

A Copublication of the International Center for Economic Growth and the
Harvard Institute for International Development

San Francisco, California

Publication signifies that the International Center for Economic Growth believes a work to be a competent treatment worthy of public consideration. The findings, interpretations, and conclusions of a work are entirely those of the authors and should not be attributed to ICEG, its affiliated organizations, its board of overseers, or organizations that support ICEG.

Inquiries, book orders, and catalog requests should be addressed to ICS Press, 243 Kearny Street, San Francisco, California 94108, USA. Telephone: (415) 981-5353; Fax: (415) 986-4878; book orders within the United States: (800) 326-0263.

Cover designer, Kent Lytle
Production editor, Lisa Silverstein TP

Library of Congress Cataloging-in-Publication Data

Guérard, Yves, 1934–
     Building private pension systems : a handbook / Yves Guérard and
Glenn Jenkins.
          p. cm.
     ''A copublication of the International Center for Economic Growth and
the Harvard Institute for International Development.''
     Includes bibliographical references.
     ISBN 1-55815-218-0
     1. Pension trusts.   2. Pension trusts—Finance.   3. Pensions.
4. Old age pensions.   5. Pension trusts—Law and legislation.
6. Pension trusts—Finance—Law and legislation.   7. Pensions—Law
and legislation.   8. Old age pensions—Law and legislation.
I. Jenkins, Glenn P.   II. Title.
HD7105.4.G83   1993
323.6'7254—dc20   92-33988
                                                                              CIP

Contents

v

Copublishers' Preface

As urbanization and industrial development accompany the rise in per capita incomes during the process of modern economic growth, new institutions are required. Security for peasant farmers in old age is provided for by having children who will take over the family acreage and care for their parents when the latter are no longer able to work. Urban employees require very different kinds of retirement security. As the economy's structure changes, therefore, pension plans of various sorts begin to appear.

Pension plans and regulations in the already industrialized world grew up in an unsystematic and even haphazard way. Firms took the lead in devising programs, and government responded in an ad hoc manner to perceived abuses. Today's newly industrializing economies, in contrast, have the opportunity to learn from the experience and mistakes of those who went before and to devise a systematic and consistent set of rules and regulations to guide and control the evolution of these funds. If the job is done properly, the immediate beneficiaries are the pensioners who live more comfortable lives in retirement, but the benefits of a well-thought-out pension system go far beyond those retirees. Pension funds are a central component in the development of a modern financial system and can stimulate and shape the nature of modern economic growth across the board.

Yves Guérard and Glenn Jenkins, the coauthors of this study, have attempted to distill the experience they have gained from helping design pension systems in a number of countries. As the study makes clear, the requirements of a complete and efficient pension system are complex. The goal is to keep the system simple and flexible; but there are important tax issues to be resolved, fund investment behavior to be regulated, and much else. Using their experience in countries that have introduced well-thought-out pension systems, the authors end their study with an illustrative draft pension law. But no country's experience is exactly like that of another, and this draft law can thus be only a general guide to the achievement of the desired goal. And a model law is only a start in any case. Making the system work in practice involves the creation of the institutions required to implement the new system.

Pension reform, therefore, is like much of the work of the Harvard Institute for International Development and the International Center for Economic Growth. One goal shared by these organizations is to help policy makers in developing countries draw from the best experience around the world with particular kinds of reform and provide practical guidelines for strengthening institutions that both encourage economic growth and contribute to general social welfare. It is then up to the decision makers within these countries to determine what best suits their particular conditions.

Nicolás Ardito-Barletta
General Director
International Center for
   Economic Growth
Panama City, Panama

Dwight H. Perkins
Director
Harvard Institute for
   International Development
Cambridge, Massachusetts

November 1992

Acknowledgments

Many people have contributed to the ideas and policy recommendations contained in this book. Catherine Prime and Graham Glenday assisted in the preparation of some of the sections in earlier versions of the work. K. Russell LaMotte provided quality assistance in research and editing that went well beyond what is reasonable to expect. The comments and suggestions of Antal Deutsch, J. Tomas Hexner, Stanford Ross, John McLean, and Marzuki Usman on earlier drafts of the book are greatly appreciated. A special thanks is due to the officials in the governments of Canada, Indonesia, Hungary, Sri Lanka, Singapore, and Malaysia who spent many hours with us in the discussion of these issues, helping us distill the essential role for laws and regulations in this area of public policy.

About the Authors

YVES GUÉRARD has spent over thirty years advising clients in the private, parapublic, and public sectors on issues of insurance, pension, and employee benefits. He is a consulting actuary with Sobeco, Inc., a major Canadian management consulting firm, of which he became president in 1975. A member of the Economic Council of Canada from 1984 to 1990 and former president of the Canadian Institute of Actuaries, he currently sits on the Council of the International Association of Actuaries. He has been active on the international scene as a consultant for the Harvard Institute for International Development (HIID) in Indonesia and Kenya and for the United Nations Development Program in Sri Lanka, where he was involved with pension and social security programs. Mr. Guérard holds a B.A. and a B.Sc. (Mathematics) from the Université de Montréal and a Ph.D. in business administration (Honoris causa) from the Laurentian University of Sudbury. He became a Fellow of the Society of Actuaries in 1963, a Fellow of the Canadian Institute of Actuaries in 1965, and a Fellow of the Conference of Consulting Actuaries in 1971.

GLENN P. JENKINS has a B.Comm. from Carleton University, an M.A. from the University of Western Ontario, and an M.A. and Ph.D. in economics from the University of Chicago. He is an Institute Fellow of HIID, director of Harvard University's International Tax Program, and the director of HIID's Program on Investment Appraisal and Management. He has held a number of other public sector positions, among them development planning advisor to the Malaysian government and assistant deputy minister in the Canadian Department of Finance. In addition, he has served as a consultant on public finance and trade issues to a wide range of countries and international organizations. He has published numerous articles in scholarly finance and economic journals on public finance, investment appraisal, economic development, and labor and resource economics.

Authors' Preface

The purpose of this book is to provide an outline of the policy issues that arise when instituting a system of private-funded pension plans. At this time, many countries—particularly those in Eastern Europe and Latin America—are rethinking their past social security policies and considering the need for new plans. While each country will have special needs and circumstances, the following represents what we feel are the core public policies required for the sound development of a private pension system that will play a major role in the development of a healthy capital market.

This book has been developed from the work of the authors in the design and management of pension plans, and from advisory services and research completed by the members of the Harvard Institute for International Development. The guidelines provided here reflect the issues faced by countries as diverse as Canada, Hungary, and Indonesia, which the authors have had the privilege to advise in the areas of pension reform and the development of financial institutions.

To add to the operational nature of this manuscript, we provide in the appendix a model pension law that contains the legal provisions necessary to facilitate implementation of the policies outlined in the text. Of course, further regulations will be required, but it is the pension law that provides the fundamental policy direction to this important set of financial institutions.

PART ONE

PENSION PLAN DEVELOPMENT
IN A MARKET ECONOMY

Chapter 1

Advantages of Funded Pensions in a Market Economy

Private Pensions and Social Security Reform

The difficulty many countries experience with maintaining public social security systems has recently attracted attention to private pension systems as supplements to (or even replacements for) public retirement income programs. Adverse demographic trends have forced public social security systems, financed on a "pay-as-you-go" basis, into financial crisis, and in some cases, insolvency.[1] Meanwhile, as populations have aged and benefit levels have increased in industrialized countries, the burden of public expenditures for retiree support, expressed as a percentage of national income, has dramatically increased.[2] It is projected that this trend will continue, with a concomitant impact on public revenue, public expenditure, and public debt. In many countries these factors have led to a fundamental reexamination of existing old-age income maintenance programs.

In response, many countries are looking to private pension systems to provide relief within an integrated system of social insurance.[3] Britain, for example, has adopted a two-tier benefit scheme. The first tier provides a public flat-rate, minimum-income benefit to which all workers must contribute, while the second tier is an earnings-related pension plan. Private employers can choose whether to participate in the second-tier public social security program or to opt out and enroll their workers in separate private pension plans, which must provide an equivalent level of benefits. It has been estimated that with roughly 50 percent of the workforce participating, this private option has reduced Britain's public social security liability by more than 30 percent.[4] Chile also has instituted a sweeping reform of its troubled social security program, replacing it completely with a mandatory, fully funded private individual pension system, which includes an optional supplemental component.[5] Another alternative being explored is individual retirement investment accounts (adopted in Belgium and France).

An increasingly important alternative (or supplement) to a public earnings-related mandatory social security system is the publicly regulated, employer-sponsored, private-funded pension plan. These plans become part of the employee compensation package that evolves over time between an employer and its workforce. Such arrangements provide for income support to the employees in old age and also assist enterprises in developing effective human resource management programs designed to improve productivity. Regardless of the degree of responsibility assumed by the public sector, governments should at least provide the correct institutional framework for private, voluntary pension plans that strengthen and complement the employer-employee relationship.

Countries with an undeveloped private pension system, or those contemplating reform of their social security systems, now enjoy a rare opportunity to design an integrated, well-planned approach to old-age income maintenance that addresses concerns of both social welfare and economic growth. This is in contrast to the United States and Western Europe, where the regulatory framework for private pension systems has evolved over time with little comprehensive or consistent direction. Partly as a consequence of this inadequacy, the massive social security systems constructed by these governments are now under severe financial stress.

Recently, international reforms have demonstrated the growing importance of private pensions in providing retirement income support. Moreover, a country's pension system plays a major role in a broad range of economic activities, especially the development of capital markets. The experience of other countries therefore suggests that close attention must be paid to the structure and regulation of private-funded pension plans in the context of social security reform. This book is designed for countries seeking to create a regulatory framework that will guide and encourage such a pension system.

The Importance of Funded Pensions in a Capital Market

The design of a private pension system has a wide-ranging impact on the development and growth of a market economy, particularly with respect to a country's financial markets. In developed countries, private-funded pensions play an integral role in the capital market. In contrast to public pay-as-you-go social security programs, funded pensions rely on accumulated contributions to finance their pension obligations. Their portfolios of assets represent a large fraction of the total debt and equity of private sector enterprises: in 1986, for example, the value of pension assets was equal to one half of the total net equity of all corporations in the United States.[6] These large, professionally managed pension funds can make a significant contribution to a functioning, competitive, and diversified capital market. We will now outline their impact on various aspects of a country's economic activity.

Source of Investment Capital and Support for Equity Market Pension funds have made substantial contributions to the stability of capital markets in developed countries, particularly in maintaining financial markets for corporate capital formation. The long-term savings structure of a funded pension system, unlike individual investment, promotes long-term fixed investments in assets such as bonds and equities.[7] Pension funds have a longer investment horizon with less concern for liquidity than other financial intermediaries or individual investors because their liabilities are typically long-term obligations set by actuarially based contracts. The growth of pension funds has thus increased the availability of medium- and long-term capital. Increased capital resources are also particularly important for major infrastructural projects and residential construction, which require secure long-term financing. The liability structure of pension funds therefore positively affects the economy's total asset-holding structure, with economy-wide advantages.

Growth and Diversity of Financial Intermediaries Private pension funds also act as financial intermediaries between individuals and their future retirement benefits. Financial intermediaries play an important role in promoting efficiency of market economies. A private pension fund subject to the incentives and competition of a private investment market will allocate its substantial capital to the most rewarding investment opportunities, particularly since information about pension fund performance is carefully monitored and publicly available. In a functioning market, those investments should correspond to the most productive uses for that capital. Unlike individual investors, who as previously discussed mainly seek security over short-term periods, professionally managed institutional investors have longer-term investment horizons. Moreover, the large size of most pension funds reduces transaction and information costs, allowing them to invest in a wider range of assets. For example, institutional investors can diversify their holdings to include assets that risk-averse individuals would avoid, such as venture capital investments offering higher rates of return (and also contributing to the development of innovative and high-tech industries). Private pension funds therefore contribute to efficient capital allocation, improving productivity and leading to growth. It must be emphasized that such market benefits depend on the assumption that pension funds, within certain limits, are allowed to invest freely to gain the highest rate of return within reasonable risk constraints.

Increased National Savings In some circumstances, the accumulation of funds in a private-funded pension system may also help generate economic growth through an increased rate of savings, leading to capital accumulation. Favorable tax treatment of pension contributions raises the net rate of return on pension savings and would be expected to raise the savings rate, particularly in cases where pension plans are mandatory. In Chile, where private pension funds account for roughly 50 percent of the nation's total time deposits, officials believe pension funding has significantly increased national savings.[8] Increased national savings in turn leads to additional capital investment and economic development.

It should be noted that some economists think the growth in private pension plans may result merely in a shift in the form in which assets are held, which reduces their beneficial impact on the savings rate.[9] Others maintain, however, that each additional dollar of pension fund contributions is offset only by a portion of reductions of other savings, generating a net contribution to the total capital stock.[10] In contrast, unfunded public pension programs such as social security may actually reduce the rate of national capital accumulation, since reductions in savings rates in expectation of social security benefits in pay-as-you-go public programs are not offset by asset accumulation.

Enhancing Labor-Capital Relations Funded pension plans also contribute to employee ownership of capital through the pension fund's stake in corporate equity.[11] This growth in widespread ownership of private firms has been cited in Chile as an important factor contributing to worker support for public policies that open up and maintain free markets, since worker attitudes toward the market system are conditioned by their stake in the investment performance of their pension funds.[12] To the extent that a private pension fund system contributes to the diversification of capital ownership then, it may also lead to increased cooperation between workers and employers in the pursuit of a productive investment climate.

Reducing the Cost of Labor Regulated pension funds also function to diversify the risk involved in maintaining income over a lifetime. Workers (and their dependents) covered by funded pension plans are assured of receiving benefits after retirement, commensurate with the duration of their employment, their salary level, and their own contributions. This risk reduction should reduce the costs of publicly funded government support and generate a net welfare gain to the population as a whole. It should also contribute to a long-term reduction in the cost of labor, which in turn should increase employment and national product.

Purposes and Advantages of Funding in the Private Pension Context

Private pension plans can take various approaches to financing their pension obligations. Under one approach, employers pay for the benefits of current pensioners directly as a current disbursement out of operating income. This is known as a pay-as-you-go system. Under another approach, referred to as a funded pension plan, employers make their contributions to a pool of assets, controlled by a separate trustee, that is designed to meet the current as well as projected benefits of pension plan members. The present value of promised future benefits is calculated by actuarial methods, and plan sponsors must contribute to the pension fund to build up assets in amounts equal to those actuarial liabilities. Funded pension plans invest the monies paid into them in order to take advantage of market investment returns, while pay-as-you-go systems simply use up current contributions to finance the benefits payable to former employees.

Funded pension plans provide significant advantages over pay-as-you-go plans for both employers and employees. Most important, funded pensions more accurately reflect the current costs of employee compensation, increase the security of pension promises to employees, and in many countries allow employers to take advantage of certain tax privileges.

Enforcement of Fiscal Responsibility As a part of the total compensation package of employees, a pension plan should reflect the actual cost of each employee during the period when he is productive. In this respect, a funded pension's current costs will more accurately reflect the firm's true current labor costs than will the current payments made under pay-as-you-go pensions. Pay-as-you-go plans defer expenses related to present employment costs to future periods when the employee is retired; that deferment tends to overstate current profits at the expense of future years.[13]

This more accurate accounting of pension costs in a funded plan gives a firm a better picture of its financial obligations and improves control of its future liabilities. Unfunded, and perhaps unknown, pension liabilities can obscure a company's real value to its creditors and shareholders. This difficulty can be resolved by requiring the accounting of pension expenses in a way that properly allocates pension costs to each year, independent of the financing approach. Moreover, pay-as-you-go methods of financing can cause more unpredictable cash-flow demands, whereas revenue requirements for funded pensions can, within certain limits, be amortized to smooth out cash requirements over time. This flexibility also improves a firm's financial position.

Increased Security Employees as well as employers have much to gain from a funded pension plan. A funded plan increases the value of a pension promise by increasing the probability that the employee will collect the pension. Without funding, the payment of pensions depends upon the future existence and solvency of the employer. A separate pension fund, however, puts funds out of reach of the employer and insulates promised benefits from fluctuations in the employer's financial stability. A separate pension fund also allows payment of the pension by a third party managing the fund, independent of the continued existence of the firm, which adds further credibility to the employer's pension promise. For example, placing pension funds in investment opportunities other than the assets of the employer-firm diversifies investment risks. This ensures the availability of funds to make pension payments when the employee attains retirement age.

The existence of funded accrued pension liabilities also makes more probable both the development of deferred pension payments and the transfer of pension rights between plans when the worker changes employers (which is known as "portability"). A deferred pension is the payment of a pension to an employee who left a firm prior to retirement. Pension payments commence when the employee reaches normal retirement age, based on the amount that accrued during his period of employment with the firm. While such a payment could be made without funding, it is more secure and more likely to be made available if funding exists.

When an employee changes jobs, pension portability between employers allows all or part of the service for the first employer to be credited to the pension available from the second employer. Since this added pension right must be purchased from the new employer, the funds from the employee's pension in some cases can be used to buy new pension rights when the employee moves. In this way, a funded pension plan facilitates pension portability.

Tax Advantages and Flexibility in Contributions Tax advantages for employers of full funding typically include an early deduction for contributions to the plan, tax-free accumulations of investment income to fund expected pension pay-outs, and tax averaging advantages gained by changing the pace of funding. In a funded system, a firm can increase contributions (within set limits) in high-profit years, and then decrease them in low-profit years. Decreased funding may be important to a firm in order to maximize the tax value of losses or tax deductions.

Increased Value of the Pension Promise Another advantage of full funding for employers is the increased value of a given pension promise to employees: the enhanced security of the pension allows employers to raise the value of compensation to employees without adding to the firm's overall financial burden. In addition, part of the pension plan may be in the form of an employee profit-sharing incentive plan, and part of the pension fund may be reinvested back into the company.

Costs of Funding The funding of pension plans also entails certain costs. The employer faces added administrative expenditures, since actuarial, legal, and investment-related expenses are all higher than the comparable administrative overhead of a pay-as-you-go plan. There is also a need to administer the funds and comply with possible government regulations. Most of these costs are fixed and, hence, are relatively higher for smaller firms. (A smaller firm would also be expected to seek a third party, such as an insurance company, to administer its pension fund and plan.) Moreover, the cash-flow demands on employers can be high in the early stages of introducing funding, depending upon the earnings and length-of-service profile of employees and whether a past-service liability has to be financed. This frontloaded cash burden can be expected to be a major point of opposition to any funding requirements. (Transitional arrangements designed to minimize these problems are discussed in Chapter 5.)

Fully funded pensions may sometimes adversely affect employees. Frontloaded funding costs may force an employer to cut back on labor costs, for example, thereby putting employees at risk of job loss or of lower cash earnings.

Chapter 2

Principles of
Pension Plan Development

Pensions are a complex area involving savings and investment issues, employment practices, taxation, and capital market institutions. An appropriate legislative framework is important to ensure the security of pensions savings, to provide effective tax treatment, and to create a role for pension plans in the development of labor and capital markets. In many countries, pensions developed long before any specific legislation was adopted. The creativity of lawyers and actuaries found ways to accommodate the new entity into the existing institutional framework. Pension laws are an invention of the last few decades. Governments were prompted to adopt such laws partly to control better the tax preferences granted to pension plans, and partly to ensure the enforceability of pension promises, which are long-term financial contracts. In a country where a private pension system has not yet been developed, the adoption of a pension law can remove uncertainties as to the legal or fiscal status of this new form of contract, thus accelerating the creation of pension plans.

It is equally important, however, that this legislative framework does not discourage either the introduction of pension plans by employers or the associated capital market developments. Where governments have attempted to impose too many constraints on pension plans, even with the best intentions, their intervention has proven counterproductive. With that in mind, we present in this section a general approach that should be followed when constructing a legislative framework for pension plans. The main components of this approach are as follows:

- Legislation should be broad and flexible.
- Transitional arrangements are needed to reduce the cost of compliance with new laws and regulations.
- Pension legislation should distinguish between long-term goals and specific short-term actions.
- Areas requiring regulation and standards must be carefully identified.
- Explicit provision has to be made for the tax treatment of contributions, pension plan earnings, and benefits.

The Need for Flexible Legislation

Different types of pension plans suit different types of firms depending upon their size, the nature of their businesses, their management styles, labor relations situations, and the salary and wage levels of their employees. For example, a well-established firm with good long-run prospects would probably establish a "defined-benefit"[14] pension plan, which stipulates future benefit levels, (typically based on the number of months of an employee's service and the employee's salary level) to encourage long-term, stable employment. Such plans deter workers with long-term service from leaving firms before retirement, since their benefits are directly tied to salary and length of service. On the other hand, a firm seeking to compete in an unstable market may prefer a "defined-contribution" plan, where pension benefits simply represent the accumulated amount of both the employer and employee contributions, plus interest. A small firm getting started might encourage employees to establish their own retirement savings arrangements.

A large firm may be able to afford the fixed costs of administering its own pension plan, whereas a smaller firm may find it cheaper to purchase a group pension plan managed by a financial institution. Some firms combine their pension plans with productivity incentive schemes, where contributions to pension plans are increased if company profits exceed a target level in a given year.

Given the diversity of situations to be covered, pension and tax legislation should be flexible enough to accommodate a wide range of employment and pension plan arrangements. Workers and employers can develop many different arrangements, each of which puts a different degree of emphasis on factors such as current versus future pay, incentive pay versus more secure or guaranteed pay, and employer-related versus individual-based savings. Over time, different types of plans can be expected to evolve as wage levels change, financial markets develop, tax incentives change, and the level of sophistication of employers and employees increases. Experience shows that the pension consultant industry, if it has the proper legal and regulatory framework, will grow rapidly in size and diversity. Unnecessarily narrow or restrictive legislation can inhibit or preclude plans from being developed that are economically beneficial to employers, employees, and the country as a whole.

The Need for Generous Transitional Arrangements

Depending on its design, a pension plan could be expensive. It can form a significant part of the wage cost of an employer. Therefore, changes in pension plans affect the entire package of wages and benefits paid to workers, and pension plan enrichment can be expected to occur at the expense of other components of the pay package.

Adverse consequences could arise if employers were required to undertake rapid changes in their pension plans, such as significantly increasing pension benefits or hastily introducing the vesting and funding of pension promises. Employers could discontinue their plans, cut their levels of employment, or, in the extreme, close down. If, however, minimum pension standards are introduced with appropriate transitional periods for compliance, employers can gradually introduce changes to their pay packages and financial structure over time. Instead of increasing base pay levels in a given year, for example, employers could choose to enrich their pension plans.

Setting Long-term Goals and Short-term Policies

In line with the flexible, evolutionary approach to pension fund development just suggested, it may be appropriate to establish a set of long-term goals that give the employer a clear indication of the status of pension plan development that the government would like to see in five or ten years. These goals could include minimum standards as well as recommended targets in such areas as the extent of employee coverage within a firm, funding and vesting levels and rates, investment composition, and levels of pension benefits.

The government could also undertake specific actions in the short term to foster pension plan development. These actions could include the following:

- establishing an annuity market
- creating tax-law provisions to foster pension portability by allowing the transfer of monies between pension funds
- establishing qualifying investment regulations for pension funds
- determining which institutions have the right to administer pension funds (large employers, insurance companies, and banks, for example)
- regulating the nature of the fiduciary relationship between financial institutions and pension beneficiaries
- training actuaries and pension plan administrators
- establishing professional associations and a regulatory body for pension plans

The Need for Regulation

In essence, employer-based pension arrangements are only one element of a labor contract. The need for regulation arises for several reasons: (1) pension savings receive preferential tax treatment, and these preferences must be limited to contain the cost of the tax assistance; (2) pension funds are administered by persons other than the beneficiaries of the fund; and (3) pension promises are long-term commitments. In such situations, regulations are required to ensure that the funds are prudently invested for the advantage of the beneficiaries alone. In practice, a significant overlap can arise between investment regulations and tax policy issues, particularly in situations where the beneficiaries of the fund are also involved in its management.

Retirement allowance plans, such as those that offer only "defined-benefit lump-sum" payments funded on a pay-as-you-go basis, require minimal regulation. They essentially represent a deferred payment of wages, and other laws covering labor contracts are relevant in this situation. When tax deferral or pension funding is present, however, more detailed regulation is required. Funding can be expected to grow as employees demand more secure pension savings, as defined contribution plans grow in popularity, or as the government encourages or requires funding to be phased in.

Tax Incentives for Pension Savings

Tax incentives play an important role in encouraging pension savings. Under one form of income tax regime, pension contributions would be deductible from the taxable income of the employer but not included in the taxable income of the employee, pension investment income from qualifying investments would accrue tax-free, and pension benefits would be fully taxable in the hands of the employee. This approach is tantamount to applying a consumption tax regime to the pension component of the compensation.

Under this system, the employer gains an up-front deduction, and the pension fund can accumulate tax-free. This deduction represents an incentive to fund a current accrued pension liability rather than to pay the pension promise directly later. While a delayed deduction would be larger than the current deduction gained from funding, the cost of the same pension on a pay-as-you-go basis would be higher, because the funds would only effectively accumulate at an after-tax return.

From the employee's perspective, this system presents two potential tax advantages. First, rather than receiving the pension contribution as current taxable income, the employee can invest this amount and let it accumulate tax-free. Second, the employer's contribution may be received as a pension when the employee is subject to a tax rate lower than when the contribution was earned, thereby generating a so-called averaging advantage. This advantage will most likely be lost if the pension is received as a lump sum rather than an annuity, since the lump-sum payment could drive the employee into a higher-than-average tax bracket, unless a special tax treatment applies.

PART TWO

THE INSTITUTIONAL FRAMEWORK OF PRIVATE PENSION PLANS

A pension law is needed to provide a framework that both enables employers to establish and contribute to pension funds and protects the benefits promised to employees once the plan is established. The pension law also needs to provide a means for self-employed people and those whose employers have no pension fund to enjoy pension benefits.

To encourage employers to establish pension funds, the procedures required by the pension law must be both simple and flexible. The law need not make such plans compulsory, but it should introduce a minimal set of standards governing the benefits that are provided. The emphasis should be on ensuring that promises, once made, are fulfilled; the pension law should *not*, however, govern the extent or content of these promises.

Transparency is safer than complexity. A simple legal framework with reporting requirements and regulatory powers is the best way of ensuring that fraud neither occurs nor remains undetected.

In Part 2 we address the institutional framework in four chapters. Their order follows the logic of the development of the pension sector. First, a legal framework has to be provided that will enable pension plans to exist. Second, benefit promises are made giving rise to commitments by employers. Third, financing for those commitments has to be provided. And finally, regulatory mechanisms have to be set up to monitor the proper functioning of the whole system.

Chapter 3
The Legal Framework

Pension Funds as Legal Entities

The existence of the pension plan must be formally recognized in the legal structure so that it may have a distinct legal personality that is capable of owning assets, receiving contributions, investing those contributions, and making benefit payments.

An employer will usually initiate the process of creating a pension plan, possibly after negotiations with the employees. However, certain employee groups (such as professional associations, unions, or trade groups) might wish to create their own plans.[15] A plan is established when a written document containing the plan rules is formally adopted and subsequently filed with a government supervisory authority, if so required. The plan rules set out the terms and conditions of the pension fund. The purpose of the pension law is to ensure that these conditions are fulfilled.

The pension plan should be seen as an instrument to carry out the pension policy of the sponsor; therefore, it is not necessary to give to the pension plan an existence completely independent from the employer in order to achieve the desired objectives. Especially in the case of medium or small firms, a less onerous approach that would reduce administrative complexities is preferable.

The fundamental requirement is that the terms and conditions must be specified in plan rules that constitute the entire contract between the employer, the participants, and the administrator. Such rules must stipulate benefits, contributions, and the powers and responsibilities of the administrator.

The Plan Administrator

A plan administrator is nominated as the highest authority of each pension plan, and is given responsibility for holding the assets and administering the fund. The administrator has the responsibility for investing the funds in the best interests of the members, for record keeping and other administrative duties, and for paying benefits in accordance with the promises. To give employers flexibility, the plan administrator should be allowed to be one of the following: the employer acting in a fiduciary capacity, a committee of employer and employee representatives, or a suitable third-party financial institution. A large employer capable of administering the plan may prefer to do so itself, or create a joint employer-employee committee. On the other hand, a small employer without these skills necessary for effectively administering pension funds would be expected to delegate the task to a third-party financial institution.

The plan administrator, whether a third party or not, should always be responsible for filing the actuarial statements, plan amendments, financial reports, and other documents mandated by law. In addition, an authorized administrator can assume the responsibility of the plan sponsor in obtaining the initial registration of the plan. This facilitates the implementation of plans in small firms, since all the paperwork can be handled by the financial institution using standard models.

Suitable financial institutions should be able to sponsor individual pension plans that would be available for purchase by individuals not covered by an employer-sponsored pension fund (self-employed people, for example). In this case, of course, all contributions are allocated to individual members, even if paid by an employer. (Individual pension plans are addressed in Chapter 7.)

Ownership and Segregation of Assets

In a funded pension plan, the amounts put aside should be segregated from the other assets of the employer so that they are available exclusively to meet the pension commitments. Employees and retirees are thus protected (to the extent of the plan's funding) against the risks to which the employer is exposed.

A typical approach is to vest the ownership of the assets in the plan's administrative body, directly or through a custodian or a fiduciary, thus putting them out of the reach of the employer's creditors and preventing the return of any part of the assets to the employer (except under pre-specified conditions). The administrator of the assets—whether a society, a committee, or an outside party—cannot use them other than to meet pension obligations in accordance with the plan rules.

Distinguishing between Employer and Plan Duties

A clear distinction should be made between the responsibility of the plan to pay the benefits to which participants become entitled and the responsibility of the employer to make the required contributions to the pension fund. A participant has no direct recourse against the employer, but the plan is entitled to contributions in accordance with the contractual funding arrangements. The provision of past service benefits upon the creation of a plan or retroactive improvements should not be implemented so as to result in a drastic drop in the net value of the employer's corporation.

Control of the Investments

The plan administrator can delegate the actual investment of the assets to an insurance company, a bank, another authorized carrier, or a combination of such third parties selected on the basis of their performance. However, if the fund is big enough, it can carry on its own investments with or without the help of outside financial advisors. When the management of the assets is delegated to an eligible financial institution that is distinct from the plan administrator, the financial institution should be responsible for preparing the financial statements, filing them, and reporting late contributions. The plan administrator should be able to rely on the third party for those duties. The pension law should determine which third parties, in suitable cases, are eligible to assume the duties of the plan administrator.

While the plan administrator has responsibility for managing the fund assets, the employer also has a strong interest in determining how the funds are invested. In a pure defined-contributions plan, the benefits promised are strictly those resulting from the accumulated contributions. By contrast, in a defined-benefit plan, future contributions of the employer depend upon the performance of the pension fund investments. For employers sponsoring defined-benefit plans, the greater the return on the plan assets, the smaller required contributions will be in the future. Similarly, the greater the investment risks assumed by the plan, the greater the risks for the employer having to make up any loss.[16]

Because of the existence of such pressures, employers often retain a dominant role in the decisions made regarding the pension fund's investment policy, either through naming a majority of the representatives to the board or committee, stipulating the investment policy, or selecting the fund manager. In some cases, therefore, the plan administrator will have no control over the investment policy. The employer's discretion should be limited, however, by fiduciary principles and investment regulations in the pension law that prevent investments from being made in the interest of the employer or of any party other than the plan beneficiaries. Insurance companies frequently will guarantee the capital and a minimum return on pension investments, which reduces the risks (and the potential gains) of the plan. (Investment regulations are discussed more thoroughly in Chapter 8.)

Administration of the Plan

Although management of the funds is an important component, the administration of a pension plan also comprises other duties. These include keeping the records necessary for the calculation of benefits, obtaining valuation reports and financial statements, making the various required filings, determining eligibility for benefits, interpreting the plan rules, and paying the benefits. The plan administrator may delegate the execution of some of these functions to a third party (such as an insurance company or a pension administrator) or to an administrative unit of the employer organization, while retaining ultimate authority and responsibility for the plan's administration.

Rights of Employees

As the ultimate beneficiaries of the plan, the employees share with the employer a common interest in the good administration of the plan and the safekeeping of its assets. Various approaches are used to represent this interest. A fairly common one is to appoint or elect employee representatives to the board or committee administering the plan or supervising the administrator. Such representation can be either mandated by law or left to local negotiations.

It is also common to guarantee that the employees or their representatives have access to certain documents such as the plan text, the financial statements, and the actuarial reports. Periodic distribution to the participants of specific information about their accrued benefits or contributions should be made compulsory.

Rights of participants cannot be diminished retroactively. Within the framework of the law, however, a sponsor can amend the plan prospectively on its own initiative because the plan was created voluntarily; this includes the power to terminate it. In brief, the employer has the same control over the pension policy as over other components of compensation. (Such control is not absolute, of course, since compensation elements may be subject to labor negotiations or informal discussions, and must in all cases be sufficiently acceptable to the work force to maintain satisfactory performance.)

Investment Regulations

The framework within which qualified investments can receive preferential tax treatment depends on the balance between various objectives. Some can be short-run macroeconomic goals, such as a limit on foreign investments; other aims could focus on the protection of the plan assets and of the participants' interests; and still others might work to prevent the use of pension plan investments for avoiding taxes. Investment regulation issues are discussed more thoroughly in Chapter 8.

Generally, investment regulations are of two types: qualitative or quantitative. The current trend is to stress the diversification of the investments through quantitative rules limiting the percentage of the assets that can be invested in any given risk (a risk being defined as one or more related corporations or real estate units). For instance, a 10 percent limit ensures that the risk is spread over at least ten different investments. The trend is to apply qualitative rules only to more general requirements, such as the application of the prudent person rule,[17] the necessity of producing an income comparable to other market investments, and the need to invest in a reasonable mix of asset types. Prescribing qualitative rules for the selection of individual securities tends to be counterproductive.

Chapter 4

Benefit Provisions and Regulations

The legal framework for pension plans can limit more or less the possible range of pension formulas. We will now examine the generally acceptable types of formulas used in developed countries today. The specific parameters can vary and are illustrative.

Benefit Formulas

Benefit promises must be explicitly specified by a written formula in the plan rules. This specificity should extend to the various conditions under which the benefits may or may not be paid. In brief, the entire contract between the plan and the participant should be set out in the plan rules (except for overriding provisions to be found in the statutory law, if any).

As mentioned in Chapter 2, there are two types of pension plans, called defined-benefit and defined-contribution plans. Their characteristics are outlined below.

Defined-Benefit Plans This approach promises a determinable set of benefits available at retirement. Typically, such a plan will stipulate that a particular unit of benefit (such as a flat dollar monthly benefit or a percentage of compensation) will accrue for each year of service. The plan sponsor contributes funds into an asset pool, where they combine with investment returns to provide resources for the payment of benefits. Under this type of plan, the future cost of the plan is determined by a range of factors, including mortality rate, age of retirement, level of compensation, and investment performance.

Two subcategories of defined-benefit plans are defined-benefit *pensions* and defined-benefit *lump sums*. Under the former, the promised benefit is a periodic payment that is typically expressed as a percentage of final average salary per year of service (for example, 1 percent of the average salary for the last five years prior to retirement per year of participation). Other formulas such as an aggregate percentage (for example, 50 percent of salary) or a flat amount are possible. The pension can be paid monthly or, in some cases, converted to a lump sum at retirement.

Under defined-benefit lump sums, however, the promised benefit is a lump-sum amount that is typically expressed as a number of months of pay per year of service (for example, three months of pay for each year of service).

Defined-Contribution Plans Under this approach, the plan specifies the level of contributions to be made to each participant's account. The promised benefit is therefore the amount that will result from accumulating the employee and the employer contributions at interest. Unlike the defined-benefit approach, no final benefit levels are guaranteed. The interest rate can be either predetermined, set at the rate earned by the funds, or set at an external reference rate, such as the rate on term deposits. Another type of arrangement that should be accommodated is a variation of this defined contribution type, where the contributions can vary in relation to a profit-sharing formula, giving rise to a profit-sharing pension plan. To cover typical arrangements, it may be advisable to add some special rules in this case.

A plan can combine more than one benefit formula type. For example, a recent trend in the United States and Canada is to accrue the employee contributions in a defined-contribution benefit formula, while the employer contributions are made toward a defined-benefit pension.

Minimum Standards

Although the pension law should not specify the level of benefits, it should set a few minimum standards for pension provisions. Minimum standards are necessary to prevent pension plans from making deceptive promises. A greater degree of regulation could limit their expansion. Moreover, as more standards are prescribed, it becomes more difficult to implement and police them. With those caveats in mind, the following areas should be covered by minimum standards set out in the pension law.

Vesting The vesting provision governs those situations where employees terminate their employment prior to retirement. Historically, pension plans were seen as rewards for long and faithful service, and less generous vesting provisions had the effect of reducing turnover, especially in the early years of employment. Currently, pension plans are seen more as a form of conditional deferred compensation or a form of insurance against financial insecurity in old age that should not be lost upon termination. This trend has led to a shortening of vesting periods.

The pension law should establish a specific period of service with the employer after which the terminating employee receives the full benefit provided by the plan formula for the period of participation already completed. Immediate vesting is not typical, however, because it results in an inefficient administrative burden and because some labor stability also has merit.

If there is no vesting in place, the employer could deprive participants of their pension by terminating them shortly before retirement. In practice, where there is some mobility of labor, the efficiency of the labor market depends greatly on the vesting provision because otherwise the benefits will tend to reflect only service with the last employer, and labor will not move to where its marginal productivity is highest.

Employers establishing plans with long vesting periods often resist shortening them, but it is possible to implement a fairly generous standard. The conditions for vesting can be based on age, service, participation, or a combination of these criteria. A simpler approach relates vesting to years of service only. Age or sex discrimination is often forbidden. Typically, the pension law requirement for full vesting varies between two and five years, depending on the circumstances of the country. If the employee leaves before this period, his or her own contributions (plus interest) should be made transferable for investment in another pension fund.

Pensionable Earnings The earnings to be taken into account in determining the base salary level will greatly affect the amount of the ultimate benefit. Issues here include whether to take into account overtime, bonuses, and other miscellaneous income. The most important factor is that a clear and stable definition be made of pensionable earnings, since the

percentage of earnings can always be set to compensate whatever definition is chosen.

Eligibility Eligibility conditions can be stipulated in terms of years of
service, age, or type of employment (full-time, part-time, temporary, or
permanent). The purpose of stipulating eligibility conditions by law is to
reduce the possibility of discrimination. Eligibility regulations could also
be used as a mechanism to limit maximum benefits by requiring their
extension to all employees. Such regulation is difficult to implement,
however, and might have negative effects on the creation of plans. One
option is to deemphasize mandated eligibility and rely on the tendency for
coverage to percolate down rather than to impose uniform conditions.
However, a balance must be sought here.

Benefits at Termination Pension regulations must distinguish between
two types of termination where benefits must be apportioned: individual
employee terminations and plan terminations. In individual cases, the full
benefits must be made available after vesting. If employment ends before
vesting, the only requirement should be the return of the employee's
contributions with interest. Benefits for individual vested terminations
are discussed in greater detail under the section in this chapter on
"Portability."

In the case of a plan termination, it is customary to disregard the
vesting conditions and credit all participants with full benefits. What is
actually payable, however, will depend on the availability of funds. The
allocation of benefits in the case of insolvent plans deserves close attention, and is discussed in Chapter 5.

Disability Benefits Pension plans frequently provide for benefits in case
of total disability. These benefits are usually supplemental to those provided by the public-sector social security system. A limited form of
benefit provision would allow for early retirement in case of permanent
disability. In the absence of any specific provision in the pension plan,
disability terminations are treated in the same way as other terminations.
We would not recommend forcing specific disability provisions on all
pension plans.

Survivor Benefits Two cases relating to the benefits that accrue to an
employee's survivor should be distinguished: death *prior* to retirement,
and death *after* retirement. If an employee dies prior to retirement, plans

can provide either for the return of the employee's contributions with interest or for the payment of the benefit as if it were a termination. If the amount payable at death is lower than at termination from other causes, a survival test should be provided for. If the amount payable when death occurs prior to ten years before the notional retirement age is defined as the present value of the survivor's pension, there will be no discontinuity in the value of the benefits. We suggest that death prior to retirement be treated as a retirement, if the death occurs within five (or ten) years of the notional retirement age.

In case of death after retirement, plans could at a minimum provide an option for survivor benefits to be paid on an actuarially equivalent basis. (Note that if death occurs after a lump sum has been paid, no additional provision need be considered.)

Retirement Age Plans must specify a normal retirement age at which full benefits are payable without restrictions. Plans may be free to enforce compulsory retirement or to allow retirement to be postponed. In the latter case, the only requirement should be that plans continue to apply the basic formula until the employee actually retires.

It is customary for plans to permit early retirement under certain conditions, with or without a reduction in benefits calculated to maintain their value equal to those payable at normal retirement. No special conditions should be required for these cases.

Indexation for Inflation Indexation refers to the adjustment of the pension payment in relation to a price (or wage) index in order to protect retirees against a decrease in the purchasing power of their pension. We limit the consideration of pension indexation here to postretirement indexation. (Note that postretirement indexation applies only to pensions, not to lump sums.)

Contractual indexation against inflation during the entire retirement period is a very expensive proposition because it requires advance funding of inflationary expectations. In most countries, private-sector employers have strongly objected to it, relying instead on voluntary ad hoc postretirement adjustments. The indexation issue is an important policy decision that depends in part on the expected inflation rate for the future. Aspects of the indexation issue are more thoroughly addressed in Chapter 10.

Locking-In and Non-Alienability

In addition to setting minimum standards for plan benefits, a pension law should address issues relating to employees' access to their pension funds. Most jurisdictions try to prevent the use of retirement savings for other purposes prior to retirement. Three principal aspects of such regulation should be addressed:

- "locking-in" of all or certain elements of pension contributions (for example, the employer's share of contributions), so that the accumulated amounts cannot be paid out prior to retirement (or early retirement)
- prohibiting borrowing against the funds, so that the benefits cannot be assigned or given in guarantee for a loan. (Using pension benefits as collateral for a loan would indirectly allow their unlocking.)
- insulating the funds from seizure so that they cannot be attached by creditors. (Attachment would also indirectly unlock the funds.)

Levels of Portability

With locking-in, an employee cannot access the termination benefits until retirement age or earlier death. Since employees do not all remain with the same employer throughout their careers, however, a pension law must stipulate what happens to employees' pension rights when their employment terminates. This issue is referred to as "portability." The general aim of portability is to link employees' ultimate pensions to reflect their whole careers, such that their pension benefits are based on participation in the plans of their successive employers.

This is a key issue for any pension system, since the existence of an efficient labor market generally requires adequate mobility. Different levels of portability can be structured, depending on the degree to which past participation in different pension plans would be recognized by new employers. Each set of termination benefits can be held by each successive employer and payment deferred until retirement age. Termination benefits can be transferred from one employer plan to the next or to an individual plan, or successive plans could fully recognize past participation in return for lump-sum transfers from past plans. These options are fully discussed in Chapter 7.

Labor Market Considerations

The mere existence of pension plans is likely to have an effect on the ability of various employers to attract or retain employees. Some of these effects can be reinforced or alleviated by the standards incorporated in the pension law. Added security and certainty of pension promises can make employees more willing to accept lower current wages with consequent gains in employment and productivity. Attention should therefore be paid to labor market policies when drafting the pension law.

Chapter 5

Pension Plan Financing: Funding Regulations and Transitional Provisions

The sponsor of a pension plan must periodically set aside assets to finance the plan's accruing liabilities. For defined-contribution plans, those contributions are easily determined by reference to the specifications in the plan rules. For example, if an employer wished to provide additional benefits to long-term employees, additional contributions would have to be made at the time the benefits were promised. Pension funding is therefore not a complex or significant issue in defined-contribution plans due to the very nature of the plan's structure.[18]

For defined-benefit plans, however, determining the rate and amount of required contributions implicates a range of issues and factors associated with pension funding. Employer contributions must be designed to be sufficient to fund the pension obligations, based on actuarial calculations of the future value of the promised benefits. Government regulations normally deal with issues such as minimum funding targets, maximum funding levels, employee contributions, tax treatment, and allocation of pension benefits in cases of underfunded plan terminations.

Another significant funding-related issue is raised by cash-flow demands created by funding requirements, particularly when benefits are improved retroactively and when new plans recognize past-service liabilities. In these cases, complete funding would require contributions not only to meet new benefits accruing presently and in the future but also to provide for the benefits accrued over past years of service.[19] Those obligations could create significant burdens for employers seeking to make contributions for both past and future liabilities all at once. Therefore, regulations should provide for transitional arrangements to minimize such distortions.

This chapter addresses the following issues related to pension funding, regulation, and transitional provisions:

1. basic issues involved in setting minimum funding regulations for defined-benefit pension plans
2. issues relating to the allocation of pension funds in case of plan insolvency
3. alternative transitional arrangements designed to minimize cash flow demands during the transition to full funding of pension promises

Basic Funding Requirements for Defined-Benefit Pension Plans

This section sets out the fundamental issues relating to pension funding for defined-benefit plans: determining contribution levels required to reach full funding, setting minimum amortization rates for unfunded liabilities, and other regulatory issues such as cost-sharing and maximum deductible contribution levels.

Distinction between Solvency and Projected Funding A solvent plan is one that, should it be terminated, has accumulated sufficient assets to discharge its accrued liabilities without further recourse to employer or employee contributions. The accrued liabilities are equal to the sum of the present values of all benefits to be paid, discounted on the basis of the expected rate of return on assets. The benefits are computed by applying the plan's formulas to years of participation and to current average pay. Solvency requirements set a floor for minimum contributions by plan sponsors.

Fully funding a plan on a *projected* or ongoing basis, however, requires more substantial funding commitments and greater fund assets. Prospective liabilities are generally higher because the ultimate benefit will be based on a higher final average pay (that is, a projected salary). Moreover, it is advisable to stabilize future cost levels, in dollars or in percentage of salaries, by building up reserves that provide for future increases in the age of the participants and thus in the cost of the pension to be credited from year to year. Therefore, a fully funded pension on an ongoing basis will require a larger buildup of fund assets than a pension funded only to the level of solvency at termination.

There is a variety of methods to determine the rate and level of funding that are required. These various funding methods differ by the extent to which contribution levels are stabilized.[20] Whatever approach is taken, however, the cost of a pension plan depends only on the benefits promised, and the plan expenses, and not on the valuation basis or funding method chosen. Under normal conditions, funding methods that provide for a faster accumulation of assets will result in lower future contribution rates. Similarly, slower asset accumulation will require higher contributions in the future. This relationship is illustrated by the following fundamental equation:

Accumulated assets
plus
Present value of future contributions
equals
Present value of future benefits

Also, different patterns of contributions will remain equal in terms of present value: if the contributions are lower in some years, they will be higher in others. Thus, changes in the valuation or funding methods will affect only the pattern for distributing the contributions or disbursements to be made from year to year, not the underlying cost of the plan.

Estimating the Liabilities The first step toward plan solvency is to ascertain the level of the plan's liabilities. The difficulty of determining these figures varies with the type of plan.[21]

For defined-benefit lump-sum plans, an accurate valuation of plan liabilities would entail discounting future expected payments on the basis of projected rates of salary increases and projected rates of interest, combined with mortality, withdrawal, and retirement rates. A simpler calculation results in a rough estimate of these liabilities, however, by adding up across participants the product of the annual pensionable salary *times* the accrued years of participation *times* the percentage credited per year of participation.[22]

Defined-benefit pension plans are more complex to value and therefore require actuarial calculations. It would be misleading to try to develop approximation rules. We therefore suggest that such plans be required to obtain an actuarial valuation when the plan becomes effective (or soon after), and at least every three years thereafter.

Determining Required Contributions (Funding Targets) Once the pension plan's liabilities are established, the next step toward plan solvency is determining the contributions required to meet the liabilities. The required contributions in a given year are normally made up of two components: *current contributions* for benefits accrued during the year and an *amortization payment* toward any existing unfunded liabilities.[23]

Current Contributions All funding methods determine a current normal contribution, that is, the amount to be paid each year to the pension fund to capitalize that part of the pension promises allocated to the current year of participation. If the fund has received such contributions each year from the onset of the plan, and the reality is in agreement with the actuarial assumptions as to interest, mortality, and other factors, then the plan will remain fully funded from year to year. A fundamental requirement is that plan sponsors pay the normal contribution each year, as estimated under the funding method selected.

Amortization Payments At any given time, there is a certain amount of accrued liabilities corresponding to the amount of funds that should be present if future normal contributions are to be sufficient to bring about full funding by the time of retirement. That amount can be calculated according to the following equation:

Accrued liabilities
equals
Present value of future benefits
less
Present value of future normal contributions

Comparing the amount of accrued liabilities with actual assets usually reveals a difference—an unfunded liability or a surplus. The amount of the unfunded liability has to be liquidated by current or future payments in addition to the normal contributions. These additional payments must be calculated to amortize the unfunded liability over a period of years, with interest. The shorter the amortization period, the higher will be the required contributions, and the plan will become fully funded sooner.

It is advisable to vary the length of the maximum amortization period depending on both the level of the funding and the source of the unfunded liability. For example, if the funds are above the solvency level, there would be no benefit reduction upon termination, even if there were some unfunded liability with reference to the target implicit in the ongoing funding method chosen. Therefore, amortization could be allowed over a longer period (such as ten years or more) in order to alleviate peak demands in required contributions. By contrast, where a plan is below the solvency level, amortization should be accelerated so that solvency is re-established quickly (within three years, for example). This can be accomplished by requiring a complete valuation report at least every three years, thereby necessitating the re-establishment of the solvency level from valuation to valuation. Giving more years to amortize a deficiency when the funds are above the solvency level will encourage sponsors to maintain a certain buffer in their funding targets so that fluctuations in fund investment returns will not bring them below the solvency level. If employers maintain their funding above the level of solvency, they will not be subjected to the more stringent cash-flow requirements that apply when funding drops below solvency.

The *source* of the unfunded liability should also be considered in determining the required rate of amortization. Where an actuarial estimation is required, for example, unfunded liabilities may arise because actual experience diverges from the actuarial assumptions (as with investment underperformance or higher-than-expected pay increases). In such cases, the unfunded liability should be amortized rapidly to avoid errors of estimation piling up.[24] A short amortization period in this case also results in more discipline in the valuation process.[25]

If, on the other hand, the unfunded liability results from the granting of benefits for past service at the inception of a plan, from retroactive improvements, or from reserve strengthening, then a longer period of amortization is advisable so as not to discourage such initiatives. In such cases, the rate of amortization should be set at a percentage of payroll equal *to the greater of* the percentage required to reach the solvency level within, say, twelve years,[26] or the percentage required to reach full funding over the remaining career of the participants.

Summary of Required Contributions The total required contributions from a plan sponsor can therefore be summarized as follows:

- the current normal contributions

plus

- the payment toward amortizing regular unfunded liabilities (within three years if funding is above the solvency level, or within twelve years if funding is below solvency)

plus

- the payment toward amortizing any ''retroactive'' liability over the remainder of the period

To keep track of the various types of payments at successive valuations, the present value of the remainder of previously established amortization payments is calculated and subtracted from the remaining unfunded liability; new amortization payments are established if necessary. From one triennial valuation to the next, all three-year amortization payments will have been made already and will not enter into the calculation.

Cost Sharing between the Employer and the Participants Many plans are contributory on the part of the employee. Some jurisdictions stipulate a maximum fraction (such as 50 percent) that can be funded by employee contributions so that there is always reasonable employer participation. These limits are often difficult to apply from year to year, however. At a minimum, there should be a rule to prevent the flow of money from the plan to the employer, so that employer contributions cannot be negative.

Tax Treatment of Funds: Maximum Deductible Contributions The tax laws should limit tax-deductible contributions to those reasonably required to fund the benefits promised under a registered plan. Therefore, only plans that do not provide excessive benefits should be registered by the supervisory authority. Limits must be set differently depending on whether the plans are of the defined-benefit or defined-contribution type. If an employer is allowed to register more than one type of plan, limits on deductible contributions should apply to the combination of all the plans. In the case of plans combining different types of formulas, we suggest a simple rule whereby the percentage of the aggregate limit used up by each type of formula is added up and the plans are accepted only if the total is within 100 percent of the limit on deductible contributions. (Limits on deductible contributions are addressed in Chapter 9.)

Allocation of Funds in Case of Insolvency

The employer's responsibility toward the plan is normally limited to the amounts he or she must contribute to conform to the funding rules. Future payments required to amortize the unfunded liabilities need not be deemed a liability of the employer until they become due. Plans can therefore be expected to have unfunded liabilities, especially if they are improved from time to time. The pension law should stipulate how pension funds should be allocated in case of the termination of an insolvent plan. Unfunded liabilities can also become a first lien on an employer's assets, but this approach would not be much use in the case of bankruptcy.

Under these circumstances, a hierarchy of benefits should be recognized. First, the obligations toward current pensioners should be covered. Then, after allocating to each current employee at least the equivalent of his own contributions (with interest), one of several alternative methods can be used to distribute the remainder:

- allocate assets starting with the older participants and fully fund the benefits credited to as many participants as possible
- allocate assets to fund a pro-rata part of the benefits credited to all participants, with or without prior full funding of pensions already in payment
- allocate assets to fund fully the benefits credited for services rendered after the creation of the pension plan, and then use the remainder to fund pro-rata any benefits credited for prior services
- allocate assets to fund a pro-rata part of all benefits after reducing the benefits that created an unfunded liability order to offset the value of the outstanding amortization payments

This order of allocation determines who is better protected in case of plan termination. It becomes particularly important in the transitional period and at any time retroactive improvements are made.[27]

Transitional Provisions: Cash-flow Problems and Conversion of Existing Arrangements

Special transitional funding provisions can encourage or discourage the creation of new plans or the enrichment of existing ones by employers. Employers may hesitate to transform existing informal benefit arrangements into an official pension plan because those promises then become legally binding commitments, which instantaneously creates an unfunded liability for which funding must start.[28] In a defined-benefit plan, the cash-flow implications of funding those increased liabilities in a single year would normally be prohibitive. Therefore, the pension law should provide for transitional funding procedures that spread such new funding requirements out over a number of years.[29]

For example, if employers maintain a plan for the future services only and continue to make payments for past services as employees retire, they will face a double burden: (1) paying the funding contributions for current service and (2) meeting the pay-as-you-go costs for prior services. This will create a peak cash-flow demand in the early years that could be avoided if employers covered the prior services under the same plan and if the funding regulations provided for the merging of the liabilities and their financing over a reasonable period. Instead of a total disbursement in the early years equal to the sum of the full normal contributions for current service and the full pay-as-you-go cost, (which could total more than twice the normal long-term contribution rate), an employer extending the plan to prior services could be required to contribute only a reasonable percentage above the normal long-term contributions. This would be achieved by lengthening the amortization period for existing plans or plans registered within a few years after the pension law is enacted, as a further incentive to the early creation of a plan.

One consequence of this approach is that a large part of the early contributions will be disbursed in payments to early or existing retirees, and the actual funds remaining to fund currently accruing liabilities will be small. If it takes twenty or forty years to finish amortizing the initial unfunded liability, it will take that many years before the pensions for services rendered in those years are fully protected. In other words, the fund will "borrow" from current contributions to pay past benefits, and if the plan were to terminate in the interim, credited benefits would have to be reduced.[30]

In order to prevent an increase in the unfunded liability, the minimum payment toward this deficiency must match the interest on it. Such a case would require the payment of the interest in perpetuity and is tantamount to a loan from the pension plans to the employer. An alternative way to ease the employer's cash-flow problem in special circumstances would be to authorize part of the payment to be made in the form of an interest-bearing note from the employer to the pension plan. This would transform part of the unfunded liability into a debt of the employer that could be gradually retired. In either case, pension benefits would not be fully secured until the unfunded liability had been liquidated, which may be achieved only after a long period.

Three further steps that could be considered to help ease the transition to full funding are: delaying the incremental minimum funding requirement, limiting minimum funding requirements to meet the liabilities of those near retirement only, or permitting investment in employer equity or debt. We will now discuss each step.

Delayed Incremental Minimum Funding Requirement This approach would introduce a minimum funding level that would require payments to increase gradually to reach the full funding rate at some future date. For example, the minimum standard could require that full funding of current pension costs only start five years after the increased liability. In other words, funding the liability for employees for the first five years would not be immediately required in full. Employers would thus have five years to gradually arrange their financial affairs in anticipation of meeting all current costs from that date onward.

This approach entails a number of problems. First, it imposes a data requirement to keep track of the past service liabilities of the employees until the catch-up is completed. Second, it has to be made clear whether or not the unfunded portion of pension payments are to be paid out from the fund or directly from the firm. If those payments are not out of the fund, then the financial demands in a firm introducing a funded system would still be the *combined* amount required to pay the still-unfunded pensions of new retirees plus the current pension costs. Hence, employers still face a large cash-flow hump unless a significant proportion of the pension liabilities has already been funded. In this case, employers could start paying a proportion of their current costs prior to the date of required funding in order to reduce this cash-flow hurdle. If, on the other hand, they can pay all pensions out of the fund, the unfunded liability may never be extinguished. Therefore, some mandatory amortization of the unfunded liability should be introduced to extinguish it eventually. This approach may thus be compounding the difficulties rather than easing the start-up.

First Funding of Pension Liabilities of Those Near Retirement Alternatively, minimum funding standards could require the full funding of past-service and current liabilities only for those employees within a given period from retirement. For example, full funding could be required only for employees within five years from the normal retirement age. Under this approach, the greatest protection would be given to those nearest retirement. The same result can be attained in a more transparent way by limiting the pension promises to a specific group of employees or calendar years of service. The formula can then be updated gradually.

Allowing Fund Investment in Employer Equity or Debt In general, to diversify risk and minimize certain tax avoidance opportunities, a fund's investment in employer equity should be limited to 20 percent at most, except for profit-sharing plans. Allowing the reinvestment of pension fund contributions into the employer's firm, however, can ease the cash-flow burden. A higher limit for fund investment, such as 50 percent, might therefore be considered as a transitional measure. This is the least satisfactory solution, but it might be the only feasible method of covering the pension liabilities arising from the introduction of a new pension plan for an enterprise with a mature labor force.

At the same time, certain guarantees should be put in place to protect plan beneficiaries against share-value manipulation. For example, when the fund sells shares, employers should be required to guarantee to pay into the fund the greater of either the current market value of the shares or their historical purchase price. It may also be desirable to limit the purchase of employer equity to public corporations with traded stocks in order to reduce problems in estimating stock market values. For other companies, regulations could be set that would allow them to hold limited amounts of unsecured debt with prescribed interest rates equal to those of time deposits of equal term. Such arrangements could be restricted to the amount of the unfunded past-service liability as of the initial implementation date of the plan.

Chapter 6
The Regulatory Structure

A government supervisory authority must be appointed to ensure that pension fund operations conform to the pension law. The supervisory authority should receive applications for registration and issue registration certificates. The pension law and regulations should also specify details that are required to appear in an annual report from the plan administrator to the supervisory authority. The supervisory authority will then have the task of using these reports to check whether pension funds are operating in accordance with the law, and also to compile statistics and information, which will inform the government of important developments regarding pension funds. The supervisory authority will also have powers of inspection, power to suspend the authority of the plan administrator if necessary, and power to terminate registration. It is better to terminate a nonperforming plan rather than allow deceptive promises to continue being made. Penalties should also be provided in the pension law for pension plans that fail to comply with regulations or tax limitations.

The Supervisory Authority

We now highlight the main functions of the supervisory authority.

Plan Registration To exist legally and benefit from favorable tax treatment, a new plan must file its original plan rules with the regulatory body. If the rules conform with requirements, the supervisory authority will register the new plan. Filing creates an independent and readily accessible source for the determination by any interested party of the provisions applying to a given participant.

The supervisory body should not become involved in an analysis of the provisions or in debating their appropriateness. To this end, the use of the word "approved," even if it is clearly for tax purposes only, should be abandoned to avoid appearing to certify the quality of the plan.

Tax Limits When a plan files its rules with the supervisory body, they should be analyzed for those provisions that bear on the maximum benefits that can be funded. The text of the plan should clearly state those maximum levels, and the application form should require the sponsor to demonstrate that the formula is within the limit.

Monitoring the Funding Process Valuation reports of pension liabilities, as well as an annual statement relating the contributions made to the required contributions, should be filed with the supervisory body. This statement would permit monitoring of a plan's funding level. It would also form the basis for checking that the claimed tax deductions are reasonable. The supervisory body should not be charged with formally auditing those statements. The monitoring should be done through systematic accumulation of the information and sample inspections.

Protection of the Assets The supervisory body should be able to ascertain that the existing assets under the control of the plan correspond to those that the required contributions should have generated. An audited statement (to be filed annually) would attest to the existence of the assets, which the supervisory body could verify occasionally on a random basis.

Monitoring Compliance with Investment Regulations The same statement should be detailed enough to enable the supervisory body to check that the fund's investments comply with regulations. It should be made clear, however, that filing does not substitute for complying with the law, and the supervisory body is not approving or passing judgment on the investments.

Verifying Benefit Payments The supervisory body should check on a random basis that the payments made by the plan are in accordance with the text. Participants should be protected against underpayments to themselves or overpayments to others. The audited statements should cover that aspect. Under certain conditions, participants should be able to ask for a check to be made.

Monitoring Plan Administration The supervisory body should be given the general power to check that plans are properly administered with respect to records, reports, enrollment and communication with participants, and other details. This power should be exercised by having systematic as well as random inspections, thus ensuring that all plans are inspected at regular intervals.

Miscellaneous Filing and Reporting In addition to the statements mentioned previously, the supervisory body should be empowered to receive any other statements that could be prescribed (such as those used for statistical purposes, for example).

Promotion of Educational Activities An important function of the supervisory body, especially during a phase-in period, should be to educate employees and employers as to the nature of pension plans, their advantages, the way they operate, and their desirable features. This activity should be an incentive, rather than coercive, mechanism to encourage more and better plans to be created.

Liquidation The pension law should not provide solely for penalties to be applied when a plan does not conform. The regulator should in extreme circumstances be given the right to seize the assets of the plan, administer it temporarily, and, if necessary, proceed to liquidate it in order to prevent fraud or other abuses.

PART THREE

PUBLIC POLICY ISSUES IN THE DEVELOPMENT OF A PRIVATE PENSION SYSTEM

In Part 3 we discuss four main areas of pension policy that will need to be addressed by policy makers structuring a private pension system:

- issues relating to pension coverage of the population (particularly the portability of pension benefits and the role of individual pension plans)
- regulations governing the investment of pension funds
- income tax provisions relating to the pension system
- indexation of pension benefits for inflation

Chapter 7

Increasing Pension Coverage:
Portability and Individual Plans

We now turn to ways of maintaining pension coverage of the population through portability of benefits and individual pension plans.

Portability of Pension Benefits

Because employees do not necessarily stay with the same employer during their whole career, special attention must be paid to what happens to pension rights when employment is terminated. The general goal of portability is that an employee's ultimate pension reflects his or her whole career: benefits should arise from participation in the plans of successive employers, not just the last one. In general, three different levels of portability are possible; these are discussed here in turn.

Deferred Termination Benefits If the vesting period is sufficiently short, most employees who leave will be entitled to termination benefits. These benefits can take the form of either an annuitized pension or a lump sum; in both cases, payment is deferred (locked-in) until employees reach normal retirement age. When employees reach retirement, they thus receive their pension from various previous employers making up an aggregate amount reflecting their whole careers.

This system does not address several problems. In particular, it leads over time to a decrease in the real value of a pension. For example, if the deferred pension is a fixed amount based on salary at termination date, its value at retirement is lower than the pension that would have been paid for the same years of participation to an employee who did not terminate. This is because post-termination inflation and salary increases have no effect on a fixed deferred pension. Lump-sum payments do not suffer the same shortcomings if a proper rate of interest is credited between termination and retirement.

Another problem with this system is that keeping track of small amounts of benefits for many terminated employees and locating them many years later often poses great administrative difficulties.

Transfer of Benefits at Termination To resolve some of these problems, the value of the benefit can be made available immediately upon termination rather than deferred until retirement. When benefits are locked-in (that is, the cash is not immediately available), the value of the pension can be transferred to a pension plan sponsored by the new employer, if any, or to a special individual pension plan if such a vehicle is provided for under the law.

This transfer procedure resolves the administrative problems, but it does not address the decreasing value problem. For example, suppose that an employee first participates in a ''one percent of average pay per year of service'' plan and that he terminates twenty years before the retirement age, after fifteen years of participation. The termination benefit can also be seen as a pension of 15 percent of his average rate of pay before he left his employment, commencing payment twenty years hence. This average is most likely much lower than what it would have been had he continued in employment, because the rate of pay would have increased due to general increases in salary levels. (Salary levels typically rise because of inflation, increased productivity, and possibly because of merit increases.)

The present value of that pension is the amount which, accumulated with interest for the next twenty years, will be sufficient to fund the payment of the pension. The lump sum to be transferred should be an amount that will make the former pension plan indifferent between immediately transferring the corresponding lump sum to a successor plan or continuing responsibility for the payment of the deferred pension when retirement age is reached. The present value should also make the pension plan of the new employer indifferent between assuming responsibility for the pension, in exchange for the transfer of the lump sum, or not receiving either the transfer of assets or the past pension responsibilities. The amount of the lump sum depends mainly upon the interest used to discount future pension payments.

If the termination benefits remain at the level described previously, the aggregate amounts that will be available at retirement will fall short of employee expectations and will tend to be smaller for mobile employees. This can be seen as a normal consequence of changing jobs and as the "price" employees have to pay for changing their career orientation. However, a more sophisticated approach can be designed for complete portability.

Complete Portability A system of complete portability would result in comparable pensions both for an employee who changes jobs and one who stays until retirement, given that both pension plans are similar. Under differing pension plans, the final pension would be a weighted average of the various plans.

A typical way to achieve complete portability is to have each successive employer's pension plan recognize equivalent participation in the previous plans in exchange for a transfer of an appropriate amount of funds. Since the ultimate pension should be higher than the sum total of the deferred pensions payable on termination, the maintenance of the full pension value imposes an increased cost that must be assumed either by the predecessor or the successor plan or shared between them. If this cost is assumed by the new employer, it becomes more expensive to hire a transferred employee rather than someone without any prior pension entitlements. If the cost is assumed by the former employer, it results in an effective increase in termination benefits for transferring employees.

Unrelated employers do not easily accept such an increased burden, but it is possible to provide for this ideal portability within a group of related employers if a policy decision is made to favor mobility within that group.

Tax Considerations Whatever level of portability is chosen, and it could vary from employer to employer, the tax law should provide for this transfer of funds between pension plans without adverse consequences.

The Role of Individual Plans in the Pension System

The self-employed and those whose employers have not sponsored a pension plan need to have some way of contributing toward their retirement benefits and of having these benefits protected. Therefore it is suggested that the pension law include provisions for approved financial institutions to sponsor individual pension plans open to the public. All contributions to such pension plans will come from the plan member, as opposed to the employer. These individual plans could also receive transfers of pension assets from employer plans when an employee leaves prior to retirement. A further development would allow contributions from employees who are already members of pension plans but seek additional retirement savings.

This individual type of pension fund provides important portability of pensions for those employees who change employers before retirement. In some cases, a previous employer may not wish to preserve a former employee's entitlement in the pension fund (due to administrative difficulties, for example), and the new employer may not have a pension fund or may not wish to accept a transfer in return for entitlement to past-service benefits. The employee could instead transfer past-service credits to an individual pension plan.

The plan administrator in such individual plans will be the sponsoring financial institution. This pension fund, like all others, will have a separate legal identity, and the individual plan administrator will have the same responsibilities as other plan administrators for investment management, record keeping and reporting, and benefit payments. The contributions will be paid into the pension fund, not into the financial institution's general asset pool. Similarly, benefits will be paid from the pension fund, not from the financial institution's general asset pool. However, assets can be commingled for investment purposes.

Special issues relating to income taxation and individual pension plans are addressed in Chapter 9.

Chapter 8

Investment Regulations for Pension Funds

This chapter focuses on some of the major issues in pension fund investment regulation. Regulations governing pension fund investments are necessary mainly to protect fund assets from conflicts of interest and to reduce tax avoidance. For example, experience suggests that embezzlement opportunities are greatly reduced when investment decisions are separated from transactions and asset custody. Moreover, given the deductibility of pension contributions and the tax-free status of pension income from qualifying investments, taxpayers can be expected to seek ways of reducing their taxes through pension investments. Investment regulations should therefore seek to limit both embezzlement and tax evasion opportunities.

Another reason for regulating pension fund investments is to control financial risk through diversification requirements. It should be noted, however, that investment regulations are not designed primarily to protect funds from financial risk. Protection from financial risk through regulation is difficult if not impossible, and depends more upon the professionalism and prudence of the investment managers of the fund. Moreover, excessive concern about financial risks can result in lower returns and hence higher pension costs. Professional investment managers normally take risk precautions, such as ensuring limited liability for any investment, as well as undertaking investment analysis. Nevertheless, some diversification requirements may be appropriate in pension regulations.

To achieve those ends, general and specific obligations and restrictions on the behavior of pension administrators should appear in the pension law. Typically, regulations distinguish between taxable and nontaxable pension fund investments. However, it may be appropriate to forbid certain investments completely. Also, specific nonqualifying investments should be clearly defined. The rest of this chapter discusses the main purposes and objectives of investment regulations.

Avoiding Conflicts of Interest and Tax Evasion

Perhaps the most important objective of pension fund investment regulation is to prevent any self-serving investments from being undertaken by the employer or fund managers. Such behavior can be avoided primarily through general fiduciary provisions such as those requiring plan administrators to conduct operations in the best interest of the plan beneficiaries alone.

There are some situations in which more specific restrictions may be appropriate to prevent conflicts of interest from arising.[31] For example, it may be desirable to prohibit completely loans from the pension plan to the employer, employees, plan administrators, employee trade unions, closely related companies, and the immediate family members of any of these persons (except where specific exceptions are established). While the use of employer debt has been suggested as a way of providing transitional arrangements for the funding of past service liabilities, low-interest loans are detrimental to the interests of the beneficiaries. Similarly, for defined-contribution plans, high-interest loans can be used as a way of exceeding any contribution limits to the plan.

Another situation is the possible prohibition of investments in the equity of the employer where this is not publicly traded, since untraded equity is difficult to value. A small business may also use this as a way of "value stripping," where the value of the company represented by the class of shares held by the plan is transferred to another class of shares. This defrauds the pension plan and can result in a further deferral of the taxation of this gain.

Promoting Diversification

The other main objective of pension fund investment regulation is to encourage diversification. The best way to deal with financial risk is by investing in a diversified portfolio of assets. A well-diversified portfolio decreases the risk attached to earning a given rate of return. One way to achieve diversification is to require that a pension plan hold no more than, say, 10 percent of the combined equity and debt of any corporation or closely related corporations. This would include the equity of the employer sponsoring the plan. (This 10 percent rate also serves to limit tax avoidance and conflicts of interest.)

It also may be desirable to put similar constraints on the size of any "parcels" of real estate (land plus buildings) that the plan may purchase. (The pension plan also may be concerned if these are not owned by some real-estate corporation, thus limiting its liabilities.) Overinvestment in real estate may also result in liquidity problems for a pension plan. Real-estate investments should be covered by specifically articulated rules in the pension regulations.

Another concern with excessive investment by a pension plan in any one corporation is that the plan may become the controlling shareholder. It is generally regarded as undesirable for a pension plan to become a channel through which the sponsor conducts various types of activities. This distracts the fund from continuously investing funds in the best interests of the plan beneficiaries. The plan can always make use of its voting rights, if necessary, as any other shareholder can. It is easier to assess the fairness of a transaction if the price is set by open market mechanisms. A requirement that a plan hold no more than 20 percent of any class of shares or bonds of any corporation may therefore be desirable.

Plans should also be discouraged from holding an excessive proportion of assets of a single type, such as land or nominally denominated debt (bonds and time deposits, for instance) whose value can be expected to move in a reasonably systematic fashion depending on changes in the economic environment. Consideration should also be given to the nature of the liabilities. Some funds seek to optimize the risk/return ratio through asset-liability matching techniques.

Another important way in which plans, particularly small ones, can diversify risk is to invest in unit funds that represent a diversified pool of assets. If such funds do not exist, ways to promote their development should be explored. These marketable, liquid assets enable small investors to diversify risk as well as to purchase indirectly the investment expertise of fund managers. These pooled unit funds could be invested in a combination of real-estate, mortgages, bonds, and equities. The purchase of insurance contracts is another effective way of reducing the financial risk for a pension fund. No restrictions on the extent of investment in pooled funds would be necessary, but the pooled fund itself should comply with the pension law and other regulations.

It is probably not appropriate to impose sophisticated diversification restrictions initially where capital markets are thin and funds may be hard pressed to find suitable investments.[32] If over time, however, pension fund managers are not investing prudently in well-diversified portfolios and are thereby putting the assets overly at risk, diversification rules may be appropriate in the regulations of the pension law.

Chapter 9

Income Taxation Issues
Relating to the Pension System

We now examine the major income taxation issues relating to the pension system. In particular, we identify problem areas that arise out of tax policy concerns or because certain gaps in the income tax may hinder the appropriate development of the pension system.

Allowing Lump-Sum Transfers and Portability

The tax regulations should provide for the tax-free transfer of pension fund assets between pension plans. Such transfers allow for both the portability of pension credits between employers when employees change jobs, and for lump-sum pension pay-outs to be converted tax free into annuities. Tax regulations could provide for three types of transfer:

- employer plan to employer plan
- employer plan to individual plan
- lump-sum pension to annuity

Treatment of Employer Debt

If the pension regulations permit employer debt to assist with the transition to full funding of pension liabilities, then any interest required to be paid on this debt should be treated as a pension-contribution tax deduction and not as a tax deduction on interest payments. This treatment will avoid unduly restricting the room available for other interest payment deductions.

Limiting Deductible Pension Contributions

In order to protect current income tax revenues, some limits are required on contributions to pension funds that receive favorable tax treatment.[33] Suggested contribution limits are set out following, according to the type of pension plan.

Individual Pension Plans Up to 20 percent of employment income per year can be contributed to an individual pension plan by an individual who is not a participant in an employer-sponsored plan. (Contributions to individual pension plans by workers also covered by employer-sponsored plans are dealt with later.)

Employer-Sponsored Defined-Contribution Plans The combined employer and employee contributions to an employer-based defined-contribution pension plan should not exceed 20 percent of an employee's employment income per year.[34]

Employer-Sponsored Defined-Benefit Plans All contributions from the employer and employees required to fund a promised benefit should be allowed for a pension equal to a certain limited percentage (say 2 percent times the years of service, or up to 75 percent) of final earnings, or the equivalent lump-sum payment. These contributions can include funding for benefits based on both past and future service.

Combined Defined-Contribution and Defined-Benefit Plans The combined value of the plans offered by an employer should not be expected to produce a pension greater than, for example, 75 percent of final earnings. It is a further policy question whether that final pension should exclude or include income from public social security programs. Maintaining this limit will require careful actuarial evaluation of the plan at the time it is registered with the appropriate government department.

Combined Defined-Benefit and Individual Plans For members of employer-based defined-benefit plans, integrating the combined benefit and individual plans would require complex calculations. It would therefore be simpler to allow at most 10 percent of net employment income to be contributed by an employee to an individual pension plan if he or she is also covered by an employer-sponsored defined-benefit plan. Conversely, it would also be simpler to limit retroactive benefits to half the defined-benefit limit for the period when individual plan contributions were permitted. This would limit the "double-dipping" that could occur when the employer later establishes a defined-benefit plan with retroactive past service benefits.

Combined Defined-Contribution and Individual Plans It would also be simpler to apply the same maximum 10 percent rule to individual plan contributions by members of employer-based pure defined-contribution plans. In other words, the combined value of all contributions to all defined-contribution plans should not exceed 30 percent of total employment income per year.

Tax Treatment of Third-Party-Managed Funds

The pension law should authorize the payment of reasonable expenses for third-party services out of the pension fund assets. Pension plan administrators can use third-party services such as lawyers, accountants, actuaries, financial consultants, and other intermediaries. Such expenses should be deductible for tax purposes.

Segregation of Pension Assets When a plan administrator delegates the management of a pension fund to a third party, special regulations are necessary to ensure compliance with tax provisions. These regulations are designed to guarantee that only legitimate pension-fund assets enjoy the benefits of tax sheltering.

A large pension fund will have sufficient assets to enable a good spread of investments to minimize the risk of loss from poor performance of one particular investment. Similarly, if the large pension fund is for a defined-benefit plan, it will be able to carry its own with regard to contingencies such as lower-than-expected overall investment performance or unexpected mortality fluctuations. It will not need any outside guarantee of the benefits.

A small pension fund is in a different position, however. Most likely, it will need to be part of a larger pool of investments so that it, too, can have the benefit of a portfolio of investments. It is recommended, therefore, that suitable financial institutions be allowed to operate "pension investment pools." These pools would be attractive to small pension funds as an investment medium and will enable them to share a spread of assets that they could not otherwise obtain.

Large plans not participating in such pools may choose an investment manager, who may be an individual or, less likely, a financial institution. In most cases, the third-party manager of large pension funds will manage the fund assets as a distinct entity, referred to as a "segregated assets" arrangement, to obtain the maximum returns.

Where pension assets are entrusted to a third-party investment manager, therefore, three different possibilities can arise:

- The pension assets are invested in common with other pension assets but separate from the assets of the managing institution.
- Each fund's assets are invested distinctly and separately from the other assets of the managing institution.
- The fund assets are combined with other assets of the managing institution.

In the first two cases, it is easy to limit the tax shelter advantages to eligible pension-fund assets. Where fund assets are combined with other third-party assets, however, significant tax compliance difficulties arise because the assets are part of a larger pool. It is therefore recommended that commingling of pension fund assets with third-party assets be prohibited.

It does not appear that combining pension assets with other assets is essential for financial institutions to be able to offer a variety of investment options to pension plans. If common funds can be set up to pool the assets of many pension plans, each plan can select a different mix of stocks, bonds, mortgages, real estate, and time deposits. Each such common fund is invested in only one type of securities and receives deposits only from registered pension plans. Nothing prevents the institution from pooling its expertise and administrative resources in seeking and managing the investments of segregated pension funds, pooled pension funds, and nonpension assets. However, if pension assets can be commingled with other assets, complex rules become necessary to isolate the earnings that are pension-related; such rules include apportioning expenses, capital gains, and interest, as well as other factors.

Moreover, investing the pension assets separately will not be much more of an administrative burden than accounting separately for pension accumulations in a common fund using complex allocation rules. From the pension system regulator's point of view, separate assets are much easier to monitor for compliance with tax and investment rules. Assets in both segregated funds and pooled funds should therefore constitute a closed tax shelter for pension assets.

Tax Treatment of Third-Party-Guaranteed Funds Small pension funds may need to buy a guarantee for the ultimate payment of benefits in case investment returns or other circumstances become adverse. When a financial institution not only manages the assets on behalf of the plan administrator but also provides a guarantee, assets attributable to the pension plan represent only the present value of the amounts payable under the contract. These amounts may be higher or lower than the assets accumulated in the tax-sheltered fund out of the contributions received. While deficits must be made up by the guarantor injecting additional monies into the sheltered fund, unreasonable surpluses that really belong and accrue to the benefit of the financial institution or its shareholders should not enjoy an indefinite tax-sheltered status, since this would extend the tax preference beyond the pension plan assets.

We therefore suggest the following rules to govern third-party-managed funds:

- Where there is no guarantee (meaning the liability of the institution toward the pension plan is contractually equal to the assets), the full accumulated assets are allowed to remain in the tax-sheltered fund.

- Where there is a guarantee of the capital, the interest, or the adequacy of the funds to meet insured defined benefits (meaning the liability of the institution toward the pension plan is not contractually equal to the assets), only assets with a market value no greater than, say, 110 percent of the liabilities can be maintained in the tax-sheltered fund.

This approach provides guarantors with an additional buffer and allows them to shelter whatever funds they have to put up in order to smooth out fluctuations against which they are protecting the pension plan. In comparison with the surplus that can exist in other funds in excess of the net pension liabilities, where the accumulated assets belong exclusively to the plan, this buffer is not unreasonable.

Thus a financial institution could commingle only those assets held for registered pension plans within a tax-sheltered fund, but each year the maximum amount that could remain in such a fund would be:

- the total of all assets under management either in segregated accounts or in pooled accounts, where the pension plan owns all the accumulated (unguaranteed) assets

plus

- 110 percent of the pension liabilities under contracts involving guarantees, where such liabilities are determined by the terms of the contract and are not equal to the accumulated assets

Accounts in excess of this total should revert to the nonsheltered fund of the institution, while the institution could transfer amounts from its nonsheltered assets to the sheltered fund to increase the pension assets to 110 percent of its pension liabilities.

Chapter 10

The Inflation Problem:
Indexation of Pension Benefits

The issue of indexation arises when the inflation rate can be expected to remain above a minimum level (say, 2 or 3 percent) over a significant number of years. Inflation makes benefits expressed in fixed terms lose their real value gradually, and in the case of high inflation they become practically worthless in a few years. Nevertheless, the issue of indexation has been hotly debated in many countries, because employers resist the dramatic cost increases indexation imposes on them. This chapter addresses the main aspects of the debate.

Inflation and Defined-Contribution Plans

Not all benefits are equally affected by inflation. In defined-contribution plans, the rate of interest at which funds are accumulated will normally include a component reflecting expected inflation that will not only preserve the real value of the funds, but will also make the real benefit grow at some positive rate of return. If benefits are paid as lump sums at termination or at retirement, inflation will present no significant problem to the participants. However, unexpected shifts in the rate of inflation result in windfall gains or losses that could become a concern if the changes are large. Large unexpected shifts in the inflation rate may also make it more difficult for the plan administrator to find suitable investments.

Inflation and Defined-Benefit Plans

If benefits are expressed as a percentage or a multiple of some average final pensionable earnings, they are inflation-proofed while the employee is a participant in the pension plan, when wages and salaries keep up with inflation. Participants in defined-benefit pension plans, however, can face inflation-related problems after retirement or termination.

Indexation after Retirement If benefits are expressed as a number of months of final average earnings and are paid as a lump sum at retirement, no problems arise for the participants (although the employer may experience funding or cash-flow problems) since the benefits will reflect an inflation-proofed earnings base.

On the other hand, if benefits are expressed as an amount payable periodically commencing at the retirement date, without any adjustment for inflation during the retirement period, inflation-based problems will arise regardless of whether the pension is actually paid periodically or its present value is paid in a lump sum. Since the fixed amount of a periodic pension calculated at retirement remains unchanged over the retirement years, its real value will decrease in proportion to the rate of inflation. A typical way to resolve this problem is to adjust the benefit amount upwards to compensate for inflation. This approach in effect stacks an indexation formula on the amount of the pension. Common indices include the consumer price index or wage-based indices, but many others can be used. The index selected and the mechanism for making the adjustment should reasonably reflect the changes in the cost of living, be readily accessible, and appear reliable to both employers and employees. It should not be open to artificial manipulation. The indexation can also be partial or complete.

Depending on the formula used to calculate it, a lump-sum payment could provide the earnings base for an indexed pension. The equivalent lump sum of a periodic fixed nominal pension should normally be the amount of capital that, if it were invested at interest, would be just sufficient to fund the pension payments as they arose. Assuming a satisfactory estimate of future nominal interest rates (which include an estimate of future inflation), both the pension fund and the retiree are put in an equivalent position whether the lump sum or the pension is paid. A higher expected rate of inflation results in a higher nominal rate of interest and a lower equivalent lump sum.

If a real rate of interest is used instead of a nominal rate to calculate the lump sum's present value, the estimated amount of the lump sum will be equivalent to including an indexation formula for the pension. The reduced rate of interest used to discount the future fixed pension benefit payments results in a much higher value for the estimated lump sum. If a retiree invests that higher lump-sum amount to obtain a return at the nominal rate of interest, he or she will be able each year to draw more from the fund than the previous year and still keep capital in the fund necessary to generate the future pension payments.

In cases where a high rate of inflation is expected, therefore, workers will sometimes prefer a lump-sum amount at retirement, which they can then invest in assets that are protected from the effects of inflation. A situation in which there is no indexation formula for the pensions, but lump sums are increased by discounting the fixed nominal pension at a real rate of interest, would force retirees to take the lump-sum option, which would be contrary to the fundamental objective of insuring income security in retirement.

Indexation and Termination before Retirement The problems existing at retirement for these workers are compounded if their employment terminates before retirement. Problems arise because in the period between the termination date and the retirement date, there is no increase in the earnings base used in calculating the benefits. As with pensions payable after retirement, the effect of inflation on termination benefits depends on whether pension benefits are expressed as lump-sum or periodic pension payments.

In the case of a periodic pension, the difference created by an indexation formula would be magnified depending on the length of the period over which it applies. In the case of lump-sum benefits, on the other hand, the effect of inflation will depend on the nominal rate of interest as compared to the rate of inflation and the real rate of wage increases.

For lump-sum benefits, the contractual retirement benefit can be a given amount expressed as a number of months of pay, based on the wage rate that would have existed at retirement. The termination benefit, however, will be expressed as the same number of months of pay, payable immediately, but on the basis of the average rate of pay at the date of termination. If nominal rates of interest are higher than average rates of pay increases, the termination benefit will be more generous than the retirement benefit. If this higher amount is transferred to the successor employer pension plan, in individual cases the liability assumed by the new plan could very well be smaller than the amount received on transfer.

This will encourage individuals to transfer these amounts to individual retirement pension plans. This option is tantamount to having no minimum retirement age after the vesting period is completed.

Summary: Defined-Benefit Plans In brief, in defined-benefit plans where the benefit is computed with reference to a final average pay, there is an automatic inflation protection until retirement or termination. At that point, the following problems arise, depending on the benefit type, if inflation is high:

- *Months-of-pay benefits (paid in lump sums).* This type of benefit is inflation-proofed at retirement (though funding difficulties are possible). At termination, a problem arises if the pension payment is deferred to retirement or if the retirement payment is paid immediately and its present value is calculated using the full nominal rate of interest as a discount rate; however, there is no benefit problem if the immediate payment is based on pay at termination without discounting, though the current cost to the employer is higher.
- *Benefits paid as pensions.* At retirement a benefit problem arises from the eroding earnings base plus the declining purchasing power of the pension as duration from retirement increases. In the case of prior termination, the same problem is made worse by a longer period of erosion of the deferred pension through inflation.
- *Pension benefits converted to lump sums.* The benefit problem here is linked to the way the lump sum is calculated: If the lump sum is the equivalent value of the pension at market or nominal interest rate, the problem is the same in substance as previously mentioned; if the lump sum is made artificially higher by discounting at a lower rate of interest, the benefit problem is resolved but the cost to the employer is much higher and difficulties of funding appear.

Arguments against Mandatory Indexation

Increased Costs In the presence of inflation, the first major consequence of adding an indexation formula is to increase greatly the cost of benefits fixed in nominal terms. However, it should be recognized that the cost of a fully indexed plan is not higher than the cost of the same plan, non-indexed, when there is no inflation. Therefore, unless employers have been raising benefit levels in anticipation of cost reductions resulting from inflationary rates of return on the assets, they should be able to afford the costs of an indexed plan, whatever the level of inflation.

Much of the resistance to the introduction of compulsory indexation focuses on the fact that it would dramatically increase the cost the employer contracted for when he set up or improved the plan, since cutting back on the basic level of benefits is politically difficult. Compulsory indexation is therefore seen as unfair, since more generous employers are hit more severely than those with less generous plans or no plan at all. However, these arguments would not apply to new plans where the rules of the game are known in advance and basic benefit levels are fixed while taking the indexation burden into account.

Funding Difficulties Another, more serious objection to an indexation formula is the difficulty of finding investments that will match the type of variation that inflation will impose on fund liabilities. Higher inflation results in wider possible fluctuations in the value of assets and liabilities. If the pension fund is not immunized against diverging values, the plan sponsor is bearing a high financial risk. This risk explains why indexed plans are more easily sponsored by governments, public corporations or corporations in a dominant position that can easily pass on the added unexpected costs in the form of higher taxes or higher prices. Many indexed plans operate on an unfunded basis, which eliminates the problem of finding matching assets.

In many jurisdictions, plan sponsors eliminate the funding problem by simply not contracting for indexation adjustments. Instead, the sponsors will pay ad hoc increases in the pension from time to time when they can afford them.

One intermediate solution is to link the indexation adjustment, implicitly or contractually, to the performance of the investment portfolio (that is, to the inflationary component of the return). If market rates of return are used, the matching problem is resolved. Because the adjustments may greatly diverge from the actual price fluctuations, however, the protection of the purchasing power may be less than adequate or short of expectations, at least on a short-term basis.

To resolve the problem of funding contractually indexed benefits or to eliminate the divergence between the inflationary component of the rate of return and the rate of price inflation, it is necessary to find indexed investments, such as indexed bonds and indexed mortgages. Equity investments such as stock or real estate often offer a reasonable long-term correlation with inflation but the short-term fluctuations are difficult to support. Short-term deposits may be useful, though they sometimes entail a lower total return. In some countries, governments have issued indexed long-term bonds that become suitable investments for indexed pension plans. Whether to issue such bonds is a major policy decision.

Complexity of Benefit Terms: Understanding Indexation

Offering an indexed pension formula is tantamount to contracting in real terms rather than in amounts expressed in the everyday currency at its nominal value. An indexed formula is therefore more complex to express, manage, and more importantly, understand, especially on the part of a participant not well versed in financial sophistications. For example, if a plan is indexed on the basis of price inflation, calculated by the ratio of a consumer price index for the last twelve months over the same index for the preceding twelve months, it is not easy for the typical retiree to verify the percentage increase or to compute the actual dollar adjustment to be made to his or her pension.

This complexity is perceived as a problem even in countries with extensive experience in pension matters. Since employees do not clearly perceive the value of the indexation feature, they resist trading a higher basic nonindexed benefit for a lower benefit even if the value is greater with indexation. This increases the resistance of the employer to spending money on a pension plan, since it lowers the return in terms of motivation or perceived value of the compensation. However, the perceived value of an indexation formula may vary greatly from country to country because of differences in past experience and cultural attitudes.

Adequacy of Pension Benefits

There is no doubt that, in the presence of high inflation, nonindexed pension plans cannot survive because they fail to meet the needs or expectations of the participants. As a result, in countries where high levels of inflation have been persistent, those pension plans that still exist are indexed or provide lump sum benefits.

As discussed previously, however, not all types of plans or benefits are equally affected by inflation. Deferred pensions credited at termination are the first victims of even moderate rates of inflation. Therefore, if there is a fair level of labor mobility, a crisis may arise regarding the portability of pension benefits, while retirement pensions continue to be marginally acceptable even without an inflation adjustment.

Defined-contribution plans are relatively immune to inflation; this is also practically the case for "months of pay" in lump-sum defined-benefit plans. Pension plans would therefore tend to gravitate toward these types of formulas where the sponsor is not willing or able to provide an indexed pension based on a percentage of pay. The choice thus may be between indexed pensions or lump-sum benefits calculated as a percentage of pay.

Employees' Point of View

For the employees, a contractual indexation formula is better than voluntary ad hoc indexation by the plan sponsor. Moreover, both these options are greatly superior to no indexation at all when inflation is significant. Therefore, at first glance, compulsory contractual indexation may appear to present only advantages for the employees.

However, because of its higher associated costs, compulsory indexation might result in far fewer plans providing for pension benefits, a lower level of basic benefits, or a reduction in compensation levels to make up for the indexation feature. The key factor is the level of inflation. At high inflation, there is not much advantage for employees to give up part of their current compensation in exchange for a worthless future pension. They would therefore prefer an indexed pension, or none at all, or another form of retirement benefits. At more moderate levels of inflation, however, employees may prefer to have a more generous non-indexed plan with a lower reduction in immediate pay, and some decline in the pension's eventual purchasing power.

Employers' Point of View

Employers would strongly resist the stacking of a compulsory indexation formula on a pre-existing plan. If the rules of the game are known in advance, however, there should be less opposition to providing indexed pensions. Moreover, if the anticipated rate of inflation is high, employers would certainly realize the futility of providing a nonindexed pension plan.

The reaction of foreign corporations may be different owing to different backgrounds in their country of origin. For instance, corporations that have fought against indexation at home and oppose it on grounds of principle may tend to carry the same attitude to foreign countries. They may also fear that the precedent created there could be used against them by their employees in other countries. Otherwise, their position should, as with domestic companies, be largely determined by considerations of costs, risks, complexity, and efficiency.

Philosophical Approach

Many people and corporations who object to compulsory indexation on the basis of principle do so on the grounds that the best inflation protection is the elimination of inflation. They argue that building indexation provisions in pension plans, securities, and other contracts decreases the will to fight inflation and effectively accepts it as a necessary evil.

When inflation persists, however, it may be unfair to let the retirees living on pensions bear the full burden of this fight, since they are no longer in a position to win an increase in their income as active employees can. Retirees therefore tend to fare worse then others in an inflationary economy because of the long-term nature of pension commitments.

A world without inflation or with very moderate inflation is certainly the better choice. But in a world where moderate inflation prevails, indexation formulas can probably make pension plans workable once their complexity is understood and accepted. At higher rates of runaway inflation, however, it is not certain that indexation formulas can reintroduce the stability in real values necessary for long-term contracts. In fact, it seems that economies subject to high rates of inflation tend to switch to barter transactions and short-term contracts.

Summary of Indexation Issues

Various options are open to a government addressing the indexation issue. It can:

- impose compulsory indexation on all plans
- impose compulsory indexation only on new plans
- impose compulsory indexation on all plans later if inflation becomes a problem
- impose distribution of excess earnings of the fund's portfolio only (a substitute for indexation)
- encourage but not impose an indexation formula
- encourage but not impose distributions of excess earnings
- take no position on indexation but facilitate it in the tax and pension laws

While more analysis and discussion of this issue are required, the dynamics of the situation where pension benefits have to compete with lump-sum benefits (which does not apply in many countries) may very well resolve the question better without government intervention. Indeed, it could be that where the benefit is expressed in the form of a pension, the plan will survive only if one of the following occurs:

- The choice is offered to take a lump-sum equivalent calculated as if inflation were moderate, so that in case of high inflation, retirees can switch to that benefit.
- A contractual indexation formula is voluntarily included by the plan sponsor to improve the perceived value of the plan and maintain good employee relations.
- A noncontractual policy of making ad hoc adjustments in case of inflation is applied consistently, and the participants trust the will and the capacity of the sponsor to continue such a policy.

APPENDIX
A MODEL LAW ON PENSION FUNDS

To translate the discussion in the previous chapters into an operational framework, the following illustrative draft pension law has been prepared. This pension law is adapted in part from the experiences of several countries that have already introduced systematic pension reform. It is designed as one illustration of the policies that have been recommended throughout this book. It should provide a useful guide to policy makers who wish to introduce such a system to promote sufficient old-age income maintenance and contribute to the development of a sound capital market.

ILLUSTRATIVE DRAFT
LAW ON PENSION PLANS

CHAPTER I

GENERAL PROVISIONS

Article 1

The definitions in this Law have the following meaning:

1. Minister means the Minister of Finance.

2. Pension Plan means any program, arrangement, or provisions that promise retirement benefits in the form of either an Employer Pension Plan or a Financial Pension Plan, and includes the funds established to provide for the payment of the benefits.

3. Employer Pension Plan means a Pension Plan established by an Employer, who is the Sponsor, for the benefit of any or all of his employees and for which he incurs a liability.

4. Co-sponsor means an Employer who has agreed to be bound to contribute to the Pension Plan sponsored by another Employer, for the benefit of any or all of his employees, with whom the Sponsor has agreed to extend the eligibility conditions.

5. Employer means an individual or corporate body or association or any other form of business employing one or more personnel in an enterprise which is under the obligation to issue compensations and who is the Sponsor or the Co-sponsor of the Pension Plan.

6. Financial Institution Pension Plan means a Pension Plan established by a Financial Institution, which is the Sponsor, to offer a Defined-Contribution Pension Program for individuals, whether employees or self-employed, other than an Employer Pension Plan for its own employees.

7. Pension Regulations means regulations containing provisions establishing a Pension Plan, drawn up by the Sponsor and used as the basis for the implementation of the pension program.

8. Participant means any individual or employee who meets the requirements of the Pension Regulations.

9. General Registration Book means the book containing a list of registered Pension Plans, including their amendments, which is kept at the Department of Finance and is available any time for perusal by the public.

10. Pension Plan Regulatory Board means the Board assisting the Minister in promoting and supervising the implementation of Pension Plans.

11. Pensionable Earnings means the participant's remuneration as defined by the Pension Regulations, on which the calculation of the contributions or the retirement benefits are based.

12. Defined-Contribution Pension Program means any program where the contributions are stipulated in the Pension Regulations without reference to the cost of the benefits, are totally allocated to the account of each participant, and where the benefits payable are limited to those resulting from the accumulation of the stipulated contributions. Any other program is deemed a defined-benefit pension program.

13. Eligible Spouse means a legal spouse or a person living with the participant in a conjugal relationship for more than a year immediately prior to the death or the retirement of the participant and that the participant has represented publicly as a spouse.

14. Profit-Sharing Pension Plan means a defined-contribution Employer Pension Plan to which the participants do not contribute, where the Employer contributions are based on a formula related to profits, and which complies with the conditions prescribed by the Minister.

15. Custodian means a financial institution approved by the Minister that, under contract, holds the assets in custody for another party.

16. Custody means a contractual arrangement where one Legal entity has possession, but not title, to another party's property.

17. Total and permanent disability means a state of invalidity that is likely to prevent permanently a person from pursuing any substantially gainful occupation for which he is reasonably prepared by his education, training, and experience.

CHAPTER II

ESTABLISHMENT AND REGISTRATION

Article 2

1. The establishment of a Pension Plan is based upon:
   a. The Pension Regulations adopted by the Sponsor;
   b. The decision issued by the Sponsor or the Co-sponsors, if any;
   c. The appointment of an Administrator and a Custodian.

2. The Pension Regulations shall be sanctioned by the Minister as provided under Articles 5 and 6, which shall apply also to any amendment.

3. A Pension Plan as set forth in this Law is a legal entity based on the authority of this Law.

Article 3

1. The Pension Regulations as referred to in Article 2 must stipulate:
   a. The formula to determine the benefits and contributions and all conditions affecting their calculation;
   b. The requirements to be a participant;
   c. The full rights and obligations of the participants and the Sponsor;
   d. The establishment of a distinct fund, separate and apart from

the other assets of the Sponsor, into which shall be paid all contributions and any earnings derived therefrom;

e. The procedure for the amendment of the Pension Regulations;

f. The Inception date and name of the Pension Plan which shall clearly identify the Sponsor, the Co-sponsors, if any, and the categories of eligible participants;

g. Any other provisions required under the Pension Law or prescribed by the Minister.

2. The Pension Regulations of an Employer Pension Plan shall further stipulate:

a. The procedure for the appointment and the replacement of the members of the Supervisory Committee, if any;

b. In the case of a defined-benefit pension program, the obligation of the Employer to pay the normal and special contributions required under the actuarial opinion filed in accordance with the standards of funding and solvency prescribed by the Minister.

3. The Pension Regulations of an Employer Pension Plan may stipulate that all contributions are paid to an insurance company which then guarantees the full payment of the benefits. In such case, the insurance contract shall be deemed to constitute a distinct fund.

4. The appointment of an Administrator as set forth in Article 2 is made by the Sponsor and shall include the following stipulations:

a. The Pension Plan's name;

b. The Sponsor's name and address;

c. The name and address of the Administrator;

d. A written statement from the Administrator confirming his agreement to be appointed Administrator, including his agreement to manage the Pension Plan in accordance with the Pension Regulations, the Law on Pension Plans, and the regulations prescribed under this law;

e. The procedure for the replacement of the Administrator.

5. The Pension Regulations of a Financial Institution Pension Plan may appoint the Financial Institution as Administrator.

6. The appointment of a Custodian as set forth in Article 2 is made by the Sponsor and shall include the following stipulations:

a. The Pension Plan's name;

b. The Sponsor's name and address;

c. The name and address of the Custodian;

d. A written statement from the Custodian confirming his agreement to be appointed Custodian, including his agreement to manage the Pension Plan in accordance with the Pension Regulations, the Law on Pension Plans, and the regulations prescribed under this law;

e. The procedure for the replacement of the Custodian.

7. The resolution of a Co-sponsor must include his agreement to be bound by the Pension Regulations and a full delegation of the powers of the Co-sponsoring Employer to the Sponsor of the Pension Plan, including the power to amend the Pension Regulations.

Article 5

1. The Sponsor submits to the Minister for his sanction a copy in duplicate of the Pension Regulations, supplemented by the decision issued by the Sponsor and by each Co-sponsor, if any, the appointment of an Administrator and of a Custodian, and in the case of a defined-benefit pension program, of the actuarial opinion stating the required Employer contributions.

2. If after examination of the sanction application as set forth in Para (1) it is found that the provisions of this Law have been met, the Pension Regulations shall be sanctioned by the issue of a Ministerial decree and entered into the Registration Book intended for this purpose.

3. One certified copy of the Pension Regulations is returned to the Pension Plan involved, while the other copy, also certified, is kept by the Minister.

4. Should there occur any differences between the two copies of the Pension Regulations certified, then the one kept by the Minister shall be considered to be the correct one.

5. In the case of an Employer Pension Plan, the documents as referred to in Para (1) shall be accompanied by a copy of the contract between the Administrator and an approved Custodian with respect to the safekeeping of the assets of the Pension Plan.

Article 6

1. If two (2) months after the filing of an application for approval as referred to in Article 5 Para (1), the Minister has not issued a decision approving or rejecting the Pension Regulations, the Sponsor may direct the Administrator to commence operations by filing with the Minister a Notice of Operation Pending Approval, stating the date at which the Pension Plan Regulations shall become effective with a copy of such Notice to the Administrator.

2. The date at which the Pension Plan may commence operations as referred to in Para (1) may not be earlier than ninety (90) days after the filing of the application referred to in Article 5 Para (1) nor earlier than thirty (30) days after the date of the Notice of Operation Pending Approval.

3. If the Pension Regulations are found by the Minister not to be in full compliance with this Law, the amendments necessary to achieve compliance shall be filed within ninety (90) days of the notification of rejection.

4. A Pension Plan may be operated pending approval during the periods referred to in Para (2) and Para (3) without contravening to Article 37, but it is otherwise subject to all the provisions of the Law and the Regulations.

5. A Sponsor may make any changes in the Pension Regulations on the basis of the procedure stipulated in this Law.

6. A change in the Pension Regulations cannot reduce any accrued Pension Benefits for Participants for the time period before such changes are submitted to the Minister.

Article 7

1. A Pension Plan becomes a Legal entity and may commence operation upon sanction by the Minister or, in the case of an Employer Pension Plan, at the effective date stated in the Notice of Operation Pending Approval.

2. The Administrator shall announce the establishment of the Pension Plan as a Legal entity by publication in the Official Gazette.

3. The sanction does not exempt the Pension Plan from compliance with the Pension Law, the Tax Law, the Labor Law, or any other Law or Regulations prescribed by the Minister.

Article 8

1. As from the date of issue of the decision to establish a Pension Plan until the date the Pension Plan becomes a Legal Entity, any right and liability arising from commitments undertaken for and on behalf of the Pension program are transferred to the Pension Plan.

2. The Custodian is responsible for the safekeeping of the assets of the Pension Plan, which assets are held separate and apart from the assets of the Custodian and shall be exempt from any legal claim made against the assets of the Custodian.

Article 9

1. An Employer may become a Co-sponsor of an existing Employer Pension Plan subject to meeting the requirements that would have been applicable at inception.

2. If an Employer who has created a Pension Plan becomes a Co-sponsor of another existing Employer Pension Plan as provided under Para (1), assets and liabilities of the two Pension Plans cannot be merged without prior approval by Ministerial Decree.

CHAPTER IV

SUPERVISION AND ADMINISTRATION

Article 10

1. An Employer Pension Plan may provide for a Supervisory Committee which consists of Employer and Participants' representatives, appointed and dismissed by the Sponsor.

2. No member of the Supervisory Committee may double as Administrator.

3. The Supervisory Committee is accountable to the Sponsor.

4. The creation of a Supervisory Committee is mandatory only if Participants are required to contribute.

5. The main duties and authorities of the Supervisory Committee comprise:
   a. Supervising the administration performed by the Administrator;
   b. Submitting to the Sponsor written reports on the results of said supervision.

Article 11

1. The Pension Regulations must provide for the management of Pension Plan by an Administrator appointed by the Sponsor. The Administrator can be a Legal person or a group of persons which may comprise representatives of the participants, acting collectively.

2. The Administrator performs any legal actions for and on behalf of the Pension Plan and represents it in and out of court. Payments made in good faith by the Administrator discharge the obligations of the Pension Plan.

3. The Administrator shall maintain necessary books and records and generally act with the care, skill, prudence, and diligence normally expected of persons given responsibility to manage the financial affairs of others. He may contract with third parties to carry out any act required in the application of the Pension Regulations and in the administration and investment of the assets.

4. In carrying out his duties the Administrator reports and is responsible to the Sponsor. Other qualifications and conditions to be met by persons serving as Administrator may be prescribed by the Minister.

Article 12

1. The Administrator is responsible for the implementation of the Pension regulations and the management of the Pension Plan.

2. The Minister may prescribe qualifications and requirements for individuals or entities to be allowed to be appointed as Administrator.

3. A Sponsor may make changes in the composition of the Administrator by appointing a new Administrator using the procedure described in the Pension Regulations, and these changes are effective upon filing with the Minister.

CHAPTER V

PARTICIPATION

Article 13

1. Any employee who is a member of a category of employees for which a Pension Plan is provided by the Employer shall be eligible to become a participant not later than the date at which he has attained age twenty (20) and completed two (2) years of service.

2. In a noncontributory Employer Pension Plan, the participation is automatic for all eligible employees. If contributions are required, the participation cannot be made compulsory for employees hired before the Pension Plan started to exist as a Legal Entity.

3. A participant cannot withdraw from an Employer Pension Plan nor claim termination benefits while he remains an eligible employee.

Article 14

1. The category of employees that shall be eligible and the moments of commencing and terminating an employee's participation in a Pension Plan must be determined in the Pension Regulations.

2. The Pension Regulations may stipulate a reasonable minimum or maximum for pensionable earnings or years of participation.

Article 15

1. The period of service of an employee for eligibility and vesting purposes is determined without regard to periods of temporary interruption of employment of one year or less. The period of participation used to calculate the benefits shall include any period for which contributions have been made by the participant, and may include years of service prior to the inception date but may not exceed the period of service.

2. Equivalent periods of service or participation with a previous Employer that have been transferred from another Pension Plan under the terms of a written transfer agreement shall be taken into account as provided for by the agreement, subject to the condition that the benefits cannot be of lesser value than the termination benefits under the previous Employer Pension Regulations.

Article 16

A Pension Plan may contain provisions under which it can accept amounts transferred from another Pension Plan, at the participant's request, within one (1) year of the date on which he becomes a participant, and can provide in exchange benefits of equal or greater value.

CHAPTER VI

CONTRIBUTIONS AND FORMATIONS OF FUNDS

Article 17

The assets of a Pension Plan are accumulated from:

1. Contributions receivable from the Sponsor or any Co-sponsor of an Employer Pension Plan;

2. Contributions receivable from the participants, if any are required under the Pension Regulations;

3. The returns obtained on the assets of the Pension Plan.

Article 18

1. An Employer who is a Sponsor or a Co-sponsor shall withhold from the participants' earnings the contributions required from them no less frequently than once a month.

2. All of the Employer's contributions, as well as those collected from participants, shall be remitted to the Administrator not later than the 15th day of the following month.

3. In case the contributions as set forth in Para (1) have not yet been paid within one (1) month, the Administrator shall demand them in writing from the Employer, with a copy to the Minister.

4. If within two (2) weeks after the demand as set forth in Para (3) the contributions have not yet been paid in full, then the Administrator shall submit a full report concerning the matter to the Minister.

5. If within two (2) weeks after the report as referred to in Para (4) has been submitted, payment of the contributions has not yet been made without any reason acceptable to the Administrator, then the full amount of the contributions, which becomes a liability of the Employer concerned, shall be declared as an Employer's debt that is due and has first priority in a court sentence execution, and is subject to an interest in accordance with the prescribed rate of interest effective as from the date referred to in Para (2).

Article 19

1. The amount of the participants' contributions shall not exceed the maximum percentage of the pensionable earnings prescribed by the Minister. A Financial Institution Pension Plan may provide for an administration fee to be collected in addition to the contributions not to exceed the maximum prescribed by the Minister.

2. The Pension Regulations of a Defined-Benefits Pension Plan may reserve the right of an Employer to obtain a reimbursement of contributions paid in excess of the amount necessary to fully fund the benefits promised. Such refund shall be subject to the solvency requirements prescribed by the Minister.

CHAPTER VII

COMPENSATION

Article 20

1. The Pension Regulations shall exclude the possibility of:
   a. Any loans with the benefits payable to a participant as security;
   b. The surrender or confiscation of the benefits payable to a participant.
2. Any transaction that purports to assign, charge, attach, anticipate, or give as security benefits payable under a Pension Plan is void.

Article 21

1. In addition to retirement benefits, a Pension Plan may provide for benefits higher than the minimum stipulated in the Law in case of termination prior to retirement, in case of total and permanent disability, or in case of death before or after retirement for surviving spouses or children.
2. The termination benefits must be such that the aggregate benefits paid to a participant, his survivors, or his estate shall in no circumstances be less than the amount of the participant's own contributions accumulated with interest at the prescribed rate up to the date the benefits commenced to be paid or the date of the refund, if earlier.
3. The benefits provided by the Pension Regulations must not exceed the maximum prescribed by the Minister under the Tax Law.

Article 22

1. The full retirement benefits accrued for participation in an Employer Pension Plan up to the date of termination must be fully vested in the participant after no more than two (2) years of participation. All contributions to a Financial Institution Pension Plan are vested immediately in the participant.

2. In case of termination for any cause prior to vesting, the value of the benefits payable shall be at least equal to the minimum stipulated by Article 21 Para (2).

3. The vested benefits accrued for participation in an Employer Pension Plan cannot be paid in cash to an employee before his Normal Retirement Age, except in case of total and permanent disability or as provided under Article 34 Para (2). In the case of termination of employment prior to entitlement to immediate retirement benefits, the cash value of the benefits may be transferred to another Pension Plan subject to the same restriction, at the employee's request, provided he survives at least thirty (30) days after the termination.

4. Notwithstanding Para (3), an amount of pension smaller than the minimum prescribed from time to time by the Minister may be commuted at the option of the Administrator and paid to the employee or, at his request, transferred to another Pension Plan.

Article 23

1. In case of retirement at the Normal Retirement Age or later, a participant is entitled to immediate retirement benefits for the full amount accumulated in accordance with the Pension Regulations.

2. The Normal Retirement Age must be stipulated in the Pension Regulations and may not exceed seventy (70).

3. In case of early retirement within ten (10) years of the Normal Retirement Age, a participant is entitled to immediate retirement benefits, subject to a reduction of the amount payable on the basis of actuarial equivalence.

4. The Pension Regulations of an Employer Pension Plan may stipulate a maximum age, greater than or equal to the Normal Retirement Age, at which retirement is compulsory.

Article 24

1. The Pension Regulations shall provide that:
   a. An eligible widow/widower shall receive at least 60 percent

of the pension payable to the retired participant, or in the case of a participant who dies within ten (10) years of the Normal Pension Age under a defined-benefit program, 60 percent of that pension that would have been payable if retirement had taken place immediately before death;

b. At the death of a participant in a Defined-Benefit Pension Program more than ten (10) years before Normal Pension Age, the benefit payable, which may be payable in a lump sum, shall be equal to at least 60 percent of the value of the deferred pension to which the participant would have been entitled if his employment had been terminated;

c. At the death of a participant in a Defined-Contribution Pension Program before the pension commences to be paid, the benefit payable in a lump sum shall be 100 percent of the amount to which the participant would have been entitled if his/her employment had then been terminated, but if the death occurs within ten (10) years of Normal Pension Age, the benefits shall be paid in the form of a life annuity payable to the widow/widower, if any can be purchased with that amount.

2. A participant may appoint a beneficiary for the receipt of any amount payable after his death, other than that payable to a designated surviving spouse, and may modify such appointment as stipulated in the Pension Regulations.

3. In case of death without entitlement to survivor benefits, or if there is no eligible spouse, the benefits payable must be at least equal to the minimum stipulated by Article 21 Para (2).

CHAPTER VIII

MANAGEMENT OF PENSION PLAN ASSETS

Article 25

1. The Administrator is responsible for the management of Pension Plan assets in compliance with the Investment Standards prescribed by the Minister.

2. The Administrator may delegate the management to a bank, an insurance company, or other institutions approved by the

Minister; he may also purchase the immediate or deferred pension, payable to a terminating participant or a beneficiary, from an insurance company that shall then become responsible for the payment of such pension benefits.

3. If the Administrator retains the management of the Pension Plan, no assets of the Pension Plan are to be lent to any person or legal entity enumerated below, nor invested in any securities issued by them, nor in any real estate used by them:

   a. the Sponsor or Co-sponsor, the Administrator, the Custodian;

   b. a corporate entity of which more than half the shares are owned by any person or any legal entity or combination of persons or legal entities comprising the Sponsor, Co-sponsor, Administrator, Custodian, union, or association of employees whose members are covered by the Pension Plan;

   c. an officer or director of any legal entity mentioned in a) or b) above and the spouse or the child of such person.

   Notwithstanding these restrictions, up to 50 percent of the assets of a Profit-Sharing Pension Plan can be invested in the shares of the Sponsor or a Co-sponsor.

4. Expenses that may be paid out of the Pension Plan are limited to the maximums prescribed by the Minister.

CHAPTER IX

GRANTING OF TAX FACILITIES

Article 26

Pension Plans established on the basis of this Law benefit from the special fiscal treatment to Pension Plans under the Tax Law.

CHAPTER X

PROMOTION AND SUPERVISION

Article 27

1. Promotion and supervision of Pension Plans is conducted by the Minister, who may prescribe by Regulations or determine

administratively all that is required to be prescribed or determined under this Law.

2. Promotion and supervision as referred to in Para (1) includes the determination of the format and the frequency of actuarial and financial reports.

3. In performing his tasks as set forth in Para (1), the Minister is assisted by a Regulatory Board.

4. The formation, function, duties, and procedures of the Regulatory Board as set forth in Para (3) are determined by Government Regulations.

5. The annual fees payable by Pension Plans and the examination fee payable upon sanction of Pensions Regulations, or amendments thereof, shall be prescribed by the Minister.

Article 28

1. The Pension Plan shall be administered so as to protect the interests of the participants and of any other person entitled to benefits under the Pension Regulations.

2. The Pension Plan must be operated in accordance with its Pension Regulations, and in compliance with the Law and the Regulations prescribed by the Minister.

3. The failure to comply with Para (1) and Para (2) is a cause for revocation of the sanction by the Minister.

Article 29

1. Pension Plans are obliged to submit to the Minister periodic reports concerning their activities. These reports shall consist of a financial report by a public accountant and a valuation report by an actuary, in accordance with the requirements prescribed by the Minister. The actuary's report shall not be required if the benefits are provided by a defined-contribution program only.

2. In conducting Promotion and Supervision as set forth in Article 27 Para (1) the Minister or an appointed official may conduct a direct inspection of the Pension Plan.

3. A Pension Plan is obliged to show books, records, and documents, and provide any information required within the scheme of an inspection as referred to in Para (2).

4. Within the framework of a direct inspection as set forth in Para (2), the Minister may appoint a public accountant and/or an actuary consultant.

Article 30

1. The Administrator shall make information available to the participants in the form and within the delays prescribed by the Minister.

2. The Administrator shall promptly inform the participants of any amendment made to the Pension Regulations.

3. The Administrator shall preserve the confidentiality of information pertaining to individual participants.

CHAPTER XI

DISSOLUTION AND SETTLEMENT

Article 31

1. The Minister may order the dissolution of a Pension Plan where benefit accruals and contributions have been suspended for more than three years. He may order the dissolution prior to that time, either at the request of the Administrator or if he is of the opinion that such action is necessary to protect the interest of the participants.

2. The Minister shall order the dissolution of a Pension Plan:
   a. upon dissolution of the Employer;
   b. if the Pension Plan becomes insolvent;
   c. if the sanction is revoked.

Article 32

1. The dissolution of a Pension Plan shall be ordered by a Decree of the Minister appointing a person or an institution, henceforth

called the liquidator, instructed to conduct the settlement. The Administrator may serve as liquidator if so appointed.

2. As from the date of issue of the Decree, the benefits provided under the Pension Regulations shall become fully vested in the participants without regard to their actual period of service. The liquidator shall forthwith notify the participants of the cessation of their participation.

3. Notwithstanding the dissolution of the Pension Plan, an Employer remains liable for the contributions required up to the date of dissolution in order to comply with the solvency requirements as prescribed by the Minister.

4. Further arrangements concerning the continuation of a suspended Pension Plan or the dissolution of a Pension Plan for any cause shall be as prescribed by Regulations issued by the Minister.

Article 33

1. All the powers of the Administrator are transferred to the liquidator upon his appointment. The liquidator has all the rights and authority necessary to conduct the settlement, which shall be completed within the period stipulated by the Minister.

2. As from the date of issue of the Ministerial decree concerning the dissolution of the Pension Plan set forth in Para (1), the liquidator may legally perform his duties.

3. During the finalizing process, the Pension Plan concerned keeps its status as a legal entity, although its activities shall be limited to safekeeping the value of the assets.

Article 34

1. The liquidator has the following duties and authorities:
   a. Perform any legal actions for and on behalf of the Pension Plan, and represent it in and out of court;
   b. Make note of every asset and liability of the Pension Plan;
   c. Determine the amount each participant is entitled to receive from the Pension Plan.

2. After the conditions have been finalized, but no later than within the delay stipulated by the Minister, the liquidator draws up a progress report recommending the procedure for the settlement of the liquidation. The obligations of the Pension Plan may be liquidated by transfer of the assets to a Financial Institution Pension Plan, by the purchase of pensions from an Insurance Company, or by cash payments to the participants, retirees, or beneficiaries.

3. Upon approval by the Minister, the liquidator proceeds to the settlement.

Article 35

1. In the event of liquidation, bankruptcy, or assignment of a Sponsor or a Co-sponsor, an amount equal to the total of:
   a. the contributions collected from the participants and not yet remitted to the Pension Plan, and
   b. the contributions required from the Employer in accordance with the funding and solvency Standards, that are due and unpaid,

   shall be deemed to have been kept separate and apart from the other assets of a Sponsor or a Co-sponsor. The Administrator shall be empowered to obtain the transfer of such assets to the Pension Plan prior to any other distribution of the assets pursuant to a court order or otherwise.

2. If the assets of a Defined-Benefit Pension Plan exceed the liabilities, no amount may revert to the Employer until provision has been made for the full payment of all the benefits provided under the Pension Regulations with respect to participation and earning received up to the date of dissolution. If the Pension Plan is contributory, before determining the excess, part of the assets should be set aside for reimbursement to the participants, if necessary, in order that no more than half the value of the benefits shall have been paid for by the employee contributions.

Article 36

1. The Minister publishes the Report of Procedure on the finalization of the liquidation in the Official Gazette.

2. The Pension Plan's status as a Legal entity terminates as from the publication date of this Report in the Official Gazette.

CHAPTER XII

PENAL PROVISIONS

Article 37

1. Whoever conducts activities of a Pension Plan without the sanction required by this Law or administers a Pension Plan in derogation to the prescribed conflict of interest rules is liable to imprisonment of at most five (5) years and a fine of at most . . . . . .

2. Criminal acts as set forth in Para (1) above are felonies.

CHAPTER XIII

TRANSITION PROVISIONS

Article 38

1. At the moment this Law comes into effect, all Pension Plans existing and already sanctioned, as well as those existing but not yet sanctioned by the Minister, are obliged to conform themselves to the provisions of this Law within a maximum delay of one (1) year.

2. The Minister may prescribe the procedure for adaptation as set forth in Para (1).

3. At the moment this Law comes into effect, funds established to provide retirement benefits to employees, in any form whatsoever, may only name themselves Pension Plans if conducted on the basis of this Law.

Article 39

This Law comes into effect on . . . . . . In order that the Law is publicly known, it is instructed to have the proclamation published in the Official Gazette.

Notes

1. These systems are usually financed by payroll taxes on the wages of current workers to support the benefits of current pensioners.

2. See Gabrielli and Fano 1986, 16, chart 1.1.

3. For a broad treatment of this trend, see Horlick 1987.

4. Goodman 1985, 107.

5. The Chilean system is described in Ferrara 1989 and in Mackenzie 1988.

6. In 1988, U.S. private pension funds held $1.77 trillion in total assets, which amounted to over 35 percent of the gross national product (GNP). Assets in private pension funds in 1988 equaled 31 percent of GNP in Great Britain, 45 percent in the Netherlands, and 22.5 percent in Canada. U.S. Department of Labor 1991, table 2.12.

7. In 1985, U.S. pensions held 65 percent of their assets in long-term assets such as corporate bonds and equities. Friedman 1986, 47.

8. Ferrara 1989, 23.

9. See Munnel 1987.

10. Feldstein 1986, 41.

11. In 1985, U.S. pension funds held almost 75 percent of their assets in corporate stocks and equities, and in the United Kingdom they amounted to 67 percent of pension fund assets. Gabrielli and Fano 1986, 28, chart 2.2.

12. Ferrara 1989, 25.

13. Trowbridge and Farr 1976, 4.

14. Different types of pension plans are discussed in more detail in Chapter 4.

15. When there is no employer, the pension plan is usually of a defined-contribution type.

16. Even in pure defined-contribution plans, however, the employer is not completely insulated from pressures resulting from benefits lower than the needs or expectations of the employees. Political pressures and paternalistic traditions will usually require some minimum level of retirement compensation for long-term employees.

17. The prudent person rule stipulates that a fiduciary such as a trustee for a pension fund may invest the fund's money in a security only if it is one that would be bought by a prudent man of discretion and intelligence who is seeking a reasonable income and preservation of capital. See, for example, the U.S. federal "prudent person rule" in ERISA § 404(a)(1); 29 U.S.C.A. § 1104(a)(1).

18. Certain elements of defined-contribution plans deserve further attention. For example, consideration could be given to allowing compulsory public-sector provident savings funds to be converted into defined-contribution plans. This would allow an individual to use these savings at some later date to buy past-service credits if they joined a defined-benefit pension plan. This provision would require special tax arrangements to allow for the transfer of funds between plans.

19. In cases where the privatization of state-owned enterprises has recently taken place, the pension liabilities from the prior service of employees might legitimately be the liability of the government rather than the current employer. In such a case, the government should recognize the liability and make arrangements for covering this obligation either over time or as part of the privatization package. For further discussion of such cases, see G. Jenkins, "Privatization and Pension Reform in Transition Economies," forthcoming in *Public Finance/Finances Publiques* (International Quarterly Journal); and Ferrara 1989.

20. For a comprehensive treatment of the alternative funding methods available, see McGill and Grubbs 1989.

21. As discussed, determining the liabilities and required contribution levels for defined-contribution plans simply entails applying the plan rules to the participant data.

22. The current cost is simply the total of annual pensionable salary times the percentage credited per year of service, minus the employee contributions and plus (or minus) the difference between the rate of interest and the average rate of increase in earnings times the accrued liabilities at the end of the year.

23. If the plan is overfunded, the surplus can be used to decrease the amount of required contributions.

24. This is particularly relevant where the government funds its past service pension liabilities (to state-owned enterprise employees) with shares of recently privatized firms. In such cases, the value of the shares might be quite uncertain. A subsequent adjustment in the funding of these past service liabilities might therefore be required as the value of those shares becomes better known.

25. In the United States, the amortization period for unfunded liabilities created by actuarial gains or losses is set at five years. ERISA § 302(b)(2),(3).

26. A twelve-year period is suggested as a conservative estimate of the average remaining career of the participants that would spread the payments over four triennial valuations; a nine-year period would result in faster amortization, and a fifteen-year period would also be acceptable in most cases.

27. However, a different priority should apply in the case of retroactive improvements, since after a registered pension plan has existed for a few years and a degree of funding has been achieved, there are reasons not to reduce it for some participants because new higher benefits are granted to others. This may not prevent some reduction in the funding ratio of earlier benefits if the improved benefits accelerate disbursements from the funds at a rate faster than amortization payments are being received.

28. Transitional funding rules may also be required when a new pension plan is introduced while existing pension arrangements are being continued on a pay-as-you-go basis for long-service employees who are about to retire.

29. Where the new plan applies only to *future* benefits and no past liability is recognized, or where the benefits of a plan are not increased retroactively, the need for transitional arrangements is greatly reduced.

30. For this reason, the rules for priority in case of plan termination (discussed previously) are of prime importance, and their consequences should be well understood.

31. Since many of these types of investment can also be motivated by tax avoidance, some restrictions may appear in the tax regulations provided that separate fiscal regulations are issued.

32. This is particularly true in countries undergoing transitions to market economies.

33. Such limits can be stipulated in either the tax laws or a regulation under the tax law, though the latter approach may be more flexible.

34. An employee's income could be calculated to include the amount that the employer contributes to the pension plan on behalf of the employee, to make this limit equivalent to the individual pension plan limit. However, this is a refinement that can add unnecessary complexities.

Selected Bibliography

Deutsch, A. 1991. "One Pension System in Transition: The Case of Hungary." Paper presented at the International Studies Association, Vancouver, March.

Ferrara, P. 1989. "The Privatization of Social Security in Chile." *Journal of Economic Growth* 3, no. 3: 18–27.

Feldstein, M. 1986. "The Case for Corporate Pensions: Some Lessons from U.S. Experience." In Gabrielli and Fano 1986.

Friedman, B. 1986. "Pension Funds, Capital Markets, and Innovative Investment from the U.S. Viewpoint." In Gabrielli and Fano 1986.

Gabrielli, G., and D. Fano, eds. 1986. *The Challenge of Private Pension Funds: Present Trends and Future Prospects in Industrialised Countries.* London: The Economist Publications.

Goodman, J. 1985. "Private Alternatives to Social Security: The Experience of Other Countries." In *Social Security: Prospects for Real Reform,* ed. P. Ferrara. Washington, D.C.: Cato Institute.

Horlick, M. 1987. "The Relationship Between Public and Private Pension Schemes: An Introductory Overview." In *Conjugating Public and Private: The Case of Pensions,* Studies and Research no. 24. Geneva: International Social Security Association.

International Monetary Fund, Fiscal Affairs Department. 1990. "Social Security Reform in Hungary." Washington, D.C. Mimeo.

Jenkins, G., and K. R. LaMotte. 1991. "Privatization and Pension Reform in Transition Economies." Harvard Institute for International Development Discussion Paper no. 401, September; paper originally prepared for International Institute for Public Finance conference scheduled for August 1991 in Leningrad.

Kopits, G. 1991. "Fiscal Reform in European Economics in Transition." International Monetary Fund Working Paper, April. Washington, D.C.

Mackenzie, G. A. 1988. "Social Security Issues in Developing Countries: The Latin American Experience." *International Monetary Fund Staff Papers* 35, no. 3.

McGill, D., and D. S. Grubbs. 1989. *Fundamentals of Private Pensions. Sixth ed.* Philadelphia: Pension Research Council, Wharton School of the University of Pennsylvania.

Munnell, A. 1987. "The Impact of Public and Private Pension Schemes on Saving and Capital Formation." In *Conjugating Public and Private: The Case of Pensions.* Studies and Research no. 24. Geneva: International Social Security Association.

Ross, S. 1991. "New Directions in American Social Protection Systems." Mimeo.

Solomon Bros. (Insurance). 1991. "European Pensions." Mimeo.

Tanzi, V. 1991. "Tax Reform in Economies in Transition: A Brief Introduction to the Main Issues." International Monetary Fund Working Paper. Washington, D.C.

Trowbridge, C. L., and C. E. Farr. 1976. *The Theory and Practice of Pension Funding.* Homewood, Ill. Irwin.

U.S. Department of Labor, Pension and Welfare Benefits Administration. 1991. *Pension Policy: An International Perspective.* Washington, D.C.: U.S. Government Printing Office.

Wachter, S. 1988. *Social Security and Private Pensions: Providing for Retirement in the Twenty-First Century.* Lexington, Mass.: Lexington Books.

The Sector Studies Series

The International Center for Economic Growth's Sector Studies analyze one country's response to a policy problem in a specific sector of the economy or compare the policies of several countries. Other Sector Studies include:

The Political Economy of Agricultural Price Intervention in Latin America
Anne O. Krueger, Maurice Schiff, and Alberto Valdés, in collaboration with Jorge Quiroz

The authors examine the effects of agricultural pricing polices in Argentina, Brazil, Chile, Colombia, and the Dominican Republic on prices, output, trade, government revenue, and the income of the urban and rural poor. The authors examine the source of the discrimination against agriculture, observing that indirect pricing policies, rooted in the national development strategy of industrialization based on import substitution, are publicly offered in explanation of this ongoing problem. But what were the underlying motivations of policy makers? The authors identify which interest groups favored which of the many pricing policies and which sectors—urban and rural, agricultural and industrial—were most affected by intervention. Finally, the authors offer concrete policy recommendations for successful price reform.

Sector Study no. 5 / 39 pp. / 1992 / ISBN 1-55815-180-X

Progress with Profits
The Development of Rural Banking in Indonesia
Richard H. Patten and Jay K. Rosengard

The authors, working with the Harvard Institute for International Development mission in Indonesia, examine two thriving rural banking systems: Bank Rakyat Indonesia and Badan Kredit Kecamatan. They compare these banks' approaches to rural lending and identify the factors that have contributed to their effectiveness. While some of the banks' success is attributable to specific circumstances in Indonesia, other factors, such as their adherence to traditional banking principles and high understanding of and responsiveness to their clientele, can be transferred to rural banks elsewhere. After years of struggling with the problem of rural poverty, development economists and bankers have much to learn from the experiences of these two banks.

Sector Study no. 4 / 114 pp. / 1991 / ISBN 1-55815-140-0

Private Sector Development and Enterprise Reforms in Growing Asian Economies
Seiji Naya

The successful economic growth of the newly industrializing countries of Asia has made them models for developing countries the world over. Naya describes many of the successful new policies enacted by newly industrializing economies to liberalize trade, promote exports, and develop enterprise potential as they become increasingly market-oriented. The author cites India's steady growth in gross domestic product in the 1980s, China's reform programs in agriculture, industry, and foreign trade over the past decade, and entrepreneurship in Hong Kong, South Korea, Malaysia, the Philippines, Pakistan, and elsewhere as examples of successful export-led growth.

Sector Study no. 3 / 107 pp. / 1990 / ISBN 1-55815-083-8

Agricultural Growth and Assistance to Africa
Lessons of a Quarter Century
Uma Lele

Based on the results of a multiyear study conducted primarily by the World Bank, this Sector Study analyzes agricultural development in Africa and the effect of external aid on its progress. Lele examines the pre-independence conditions, the developmental progress and history, and the political stability of Kenya, Malawi, and Tanzania in East Africa and of Cameroon, Nigeria, and Senegal in West Africa. Among the issues addressed are whether aid can be targeted more effectively and more efficiently and what information donors and recipients must have to formulate the best assistance strategies and programs.

Sector Study no. 2 / 106 pp. / 1990 / ISBN 1-55815-063-3

Linkages in Developing Economies
A Philippine Study
Gustav Ranis, Frances Stewart, and Edna Angeles-Reyes

The authors examine linkages between the agricultural and nonagricultural sectors in the Philippines. They integrate micro and macro approaches to determine how these linkages influence overall development and find that both high geographic concentration of development and high industrial concentration are related to weak rural linkages. Both types of concentration are due to import substitution, lack of infrastructure in some areas, and inequality, which creates inappropriate demands for products that can only be imported or are capital intensive.

Sector Study no. 1 / 87 pp. / 1990 / ISBN 1-55815-049-8

ICEG Academic Advisory Board